A FIELD GUIDE TO SHARING YOUR FAITH

Greg Stier

D2S Publishing

Dare 2 Share

Copyright © 2006, 2010, 2011, by Dare 2 Share Ministries, Inc.
Revised and updated.
All rights reserved.
The GOSPEL Journey is a registered trademark of Dare 2 Share Ministries.

A D2S Publishing book
PO Box 745323
Arvada, CO 80006

Editor: Jane Dratz
Stier, Greg.

Dare 2 Share: a field guide to sharing your faith with anyone, anytime, anywhere!

ISBN: 978-0-9827733-0-7

Library of Congress Control Number: 2011923946

Printed in the United States of America

1 2 3 4 5 6 7 8 9 /

*To Jeremy, the little boy who melts my heart
and makes me laugh, may you grow in the love of Jesus
and have a passion to tell everyone about Him.*

TABLE OF CONTENTS

Part One: Getting Ready for the Journey

Part Two: Sharing Your Faith

Part Three: Reaching Other Worldviews

ACKNOWLEDGMENTS

I am so grateful for the help that Jane Dratz provided for this second edition of the *Dare 2 Share Field Guide*. Jane worked hard to balance the relentless and relational aspects of this book in a way that far surpasses the first edition. As always, her super-relational bent provided a great counterbalance to my super-relentless approach to evangelism. The results are a book that equips teenagers to speak the truth in love to their friends with their lives and their lips. Thank you, Jane.

Lane, thanks for the hard work you put into part 3 of this book. Your research was excellent and your witty, sometimes sarcastic, and always insightful comments make this section especially powerful and practical.

Finally, thanks to the entire Dare 2 Share team. Your hard work and dedication is resulting in a generation of teenagers being mobilized to reach their friends, classmates and teammates with the good news of Jesus Christ!

READ THIS FIRST

This book is not designed to sit on your shelf or to exist under a pile of clothes in your room. It is designed to be a field guide to sharing your faith with your friends. I encourage you to read it through once to get the faith-sharing basics down, but after that, put it in your backpack and take it with you to school. You'll find it's a ready reference when you're wondering how to get the conversation started with your Mormon friend at lunch or wanting to take the next step with your friend who's an atheist. Just flip to the back of the book and read up for a minute or two and you'll find loads of ideas tailored to specific belief systems to help you share Jesus in a relevant and nonthreatening way, including:

- Agnosticism
- Atheism
- Buddhism
- Hinduism
- The Watchtower and Track Society (Jehovah's Witnesses)
- Judaism
- Mormonism
- Islam (Muslim beliefs)
- Wicca (a form of witchcraft)
- And more!

But what you are not going to find in the back of this book are some kind of spiritual bullets that you can lock and load into your gospel "gun" to blow them away with! Instead, you'll find conversation starters, compliments and common ground, the areas you probably agree on and disagree about, a few key passages to focus on in your talk, and some helpful hints. Part 3 includes more in-depth information about what each of these belief systems hold to and how they often differ from the essentials of Christianity.

But this field guide doesn't stop there. As you read this book you'll also discover the following:

- How to identify your style of sharing Jesus
- How to lay the groundwork through prayer
- How to initiate spiritual conversations with your friends
- How to share the gospel message in a clear and compassionate way
- How to share your own personal story of coming to believe in Jesus
- And much, much more!

When you're done reading this book and learning the principles it explains, you'll know how to share your faith anytime, anywhere, with anyone!

This book will also help you realize that one of the most powerful persuaders when it comes to sharing Jesus is a Spirit-empowered, loving Christian who listens just as much as he or she talks!

Along the way there are some short and helpful parts of this book that will give you insights, information, and encouragement for sharing Jesus with your friends:

Warning!

This section will give you a heads-up to help you avoid some common mistakes others have made when sharing Jesus with friends.

True Confessions

Here's where I share a true story from my own experiences where I messed up sharing the gospel with somebody else.

Can I Get a Witness?

These are true stories or insights from teenagers who are daring to share their faith anytime, anywhere, and with anyone.

Evangetips

These will give you some tactical and practical help regarding websites, resources, and ideas to help you become better at sharing your faith with your friends.

So before you get started, realize that when you share Jesus with your friends you are taking them on the journey of a lifetime. This book can become your field guide during this dangerous and exciting adventure. Of course the ultimate field guide is the Word of God itself!

My challenge to you is to read *Dare 2 Share* all the way through once. Take a few hours, sit down, and read the whole thing (believe me, it's easy reading!). Then put it in your backpack to keep with you as a handy reference guide. This will give you easy access to the basic information you need to share your faith with anyone, anytime, anywhere!

But more than anything else, before you get started, pray. Pray that God will move in your heart, soul, and mind to give you the passionate motivation and the practical tools to reach your friends, family, classmates, teammates, and coworkers for Jesus. This life-changing adventure will not only transform your friends, it will change you on the deepest level as well.

Let the journey begin right now!

PART ONE:
GETTING READY FOR THE JOURNEY

chapter 1

HOW TO BE MORE LIKE JESUS

Do you want to be more like Jesus? Do you *really*?

I challenge myself with this question all the time. And in my better moments, I answer it with a resounding "Yes!" I'm guessing that you do to. After all, who wouldn't want to be like Jesus? He fed the hungry, healed the sick, passed out good advice, knew how to gather a crowd, walked on water and did all sorts of amazing stuff.

But for you and I to be like Jesus, to *really* be like Jesus, we need to look beyond all the cool things Jesus did and get a feel for what motivated Him to do what He did. What made His heart burn and break?

What I've discovered as I've searched for the answer to this question and poured over Jesus' life in the gospels is that what motivated Jesus to live like He lived was His heart for the lost.

You see, while Jesus walked this earth He was on a desperate search and rescue mission for the lost. Check out His words in Luke 19:10: "For the Son of Man came to seek and to save what was lost." It's clear that this was the passion and focus of His life—it was His cause.

Did you know that Jesus has called us to this same cause? He passed His cause along to us, His followers, right before He ascended into Heaven when He commanded us to "go and make disciples" (Matthew 28:19).

So to be like Jesus, to *really* be like Him, we must cultivate hearts that burn and break for the lost. We must join His search and rescue mission. We must reach out to those who need Jesus, starting with our own friends, teammates and classmates. Christ's cause of seeking and saving the lost is THE Cause that should capture our passion and focus our lives.

I'm talking about a *desperate* search and rescue mission. Have you ever lost something very important to you? I have. I can't help but think about when I lost my little four year old girl at Disney World. It was a hot and muggy day in Orlando. To be honest, I thought I had a foolproof way of making sure I didn't lose my kids in the hustle-bustle mayhem of all things Mickey. My child retention "technique" was making sure I kept my hand on her back all day as we walked through the crowds. Sure, I could have carried her (but I was tired), rented a child stroller (but I was broke) or used a child leash (but I have limits), but I chose the hand/back method.

It was all working fine until I looked down one time and realized I was gently guiding the wrong little girl around. Needless to say, I freaked out. Not only did I lose my girl, but now I was going to jail! I quickly located the girl's father (who was only a few feet away) and apologized. And then I went on a desperate search for my little girl. My heart pounded, the sweat poured even more. It was probably only a minute or so before I located my little girl, but in that minute time slowed down and my mind raced. I ran around like a crazy man looking for my little girl, calling out "Kailey!!! Kailey!!! Kailey!!!" When I finally found her the joy and relief in my heart was indescribable.

This story may give you a taste of the degree of intensity surging in the heart of Jesus as He accomplishes His search and rescue mission for souls. He is inviting us into this holy quest. If we really want to be like Jesus then we have to be willing to drop everything else and call out to lost souls who are lost in the crowd, who are lost in this life and doomed in the next apart from Jesus Christ.

But let's be honest, sometimes just the thought of reaching out to those who need Jesus feels overwhelming and makes us wonder if it's really worth it.

CARRYING HIS MESSAGE OF HOPE AND LIFE

In the busyness of classes, clubs, sports and friends, it can be hard to wrap our minds around the amazing truth that we have the message of hope and life others need. But when you stop and really think about it, nothing else in this world compares to this hope you and I carry in our souls! It's the most important message on the planet—and Jesus has entrusted it to you and me! Each of us has been given the privilege of passing His message on by reaching out to those in our circle of influence with His good news of love, forgiveness, salvation and eternal life.

In fact, sharing Jesus' message with others is the most impacting thing we will ever, ever do. Sharing Jesus is more life changing than winning the lottery. It carries more punch than giving away a million dollars to a worthy cause. It's more world transforming than finding the cure to cancer. Because sharing

Jesus with those who don't know Him can change someone's life at the deepest level—both now and for all eternity. And nothing else we could ever be involved in is more significant than that! That's why this cause Jesus has called us to is THE Cause of all causes—making disciples who make disciples.

This book is about more than just making "converts" to Christianity. It's about making fully surrendered followers of Jesus (AKA "Disciples") who spiritually reproduce producers who reproduce. But that often painful, always time-intensive and truly exciting process all begins with sharing the good news of Jesus with someone else. If you can't do that, then you can't make disciples who make disciples. And all of this starts with a relationship.

At its core, Jesus' message is about a relationship with God, not about a religion of rules and regulations. It's about a free gift, not about trying to earn your way to heaven. It's about living the life God's given you to the fullest, according to His blueprint for a satisfying, meaningful life, so that you might know Him and make Him known. That's why the Bible calls it "Good News"! So yes, it is *really* worth it!

And who better than you to reach your friends?

THE POWER OF RELATIONSHIP

Did you know that as a friend you have one hundred times more influence on your friends than a stranger does?[1] That means that you have the potential to impact your friends for Jesus far more significantly than any stranger ever could. In fact, I believe God has purposefully planted you in your circle of influence so you can reach into your friends' lives with Jesus' love and His gospel message. Because every teen deserves to hear about God's grace and love from another teen they know and respect.

Think of it! If you *really* want to be like Jesus, you have the message of hope and you have the potential to influence your friends to consider Jesus.

STEPPING UP TO THE CHALLENGE

But even if you're willing to step up to the challenge and the call, maybe you feel like you don't know where to start when it comes to talking to your friends about Jesus. Well, that's what this book is all about—motivating and mobilizing you to share your faith. This field guide will give you the tools, encouragement and insights you need to join THE Cause and begin the process of making disciples who make disciples.

You'll learn how to initiate spiritual conversations that are relevant and respectful. You'll learn how to use compliments and common ground to move the conversation toward Jesus. You'll learn how to explain the gospel to your friends in a way that is clear and compelling.

So get ready! You're about to launch into the exciting, and sometimes intimidating, adventure of becoming more like Jesus by daring to share your faith with your friends.

chapter 2

HOW TO GET MOTIVATED

Sharing Jesus all starts with passion. Without a passion to share your faith you won't bother to learn how; you'll probably quit after the first failed attempt. It's passion for Jesus and for those who don't know Him that will give you the fuel you need to share your faith. I call this internal drive and motivation that gets our motors running for THE Cause of Christ "passion fuel."

How do you get passion fuel in your spiritual system? You ask God for it. You search God's Word for it. You seek it with all your heart. Ultimately, it's passion fuel that makes your heart burn and beat for the lost.

PASSION FUEL

When you stop to think about it, you see motivational fuel everywhere. If you have a friend who is really good at sports and excels on the court or the field, he or she is probably charged up on passion fuel. That is the burning, brewing motivation that sizzles and simmers behind their athletic accomplishments.

For some that passion fuel is comprised of a longing to hear "Way to go!" or "I'm proud of you!" from their dad. For some it is jealousy that fuels their actions. For others it is the desire for a scholarship or popularity at their school.

There are all sorts of motivations that can comprise passion fuel, good ones or bad ones. The point is that everyone who excels at anything is usually propelled by fuel of some brand.

Although I was never a very good basketball player in middle school, I was on the Red-Bull-meets-5-hour-ENERGY form of passion fuel. What motivated me? I wanted to please Coach Adams. Never having a dad in my life, this former Kentucky Wildcat basketball player became an immediate father figure to me. What he valued was "hustle," not talent. He described hustle as leaving it all on the court. Running harder, fighting for rebounds, diving for loose basketballs were all part of the hustle factor. So, although I was the most uncoordinated player on the team, I refused to be outworked. I remember Coach Adams telling the other players, "Take a look at Stier over here. He ain't got an ounce of athletic ability. He may be running down the court the wrong way, but he's running hard. If you had half the heart Stier did, we'd win every game!" Although I never scored more than ten points in a game, I was fueled by the thought of hearing "Way to hustle, Stier," from Coach Adams. I still have the yearbook where he wrote, "Greg, I appreciate your hustle!" Throughout my high school years whenever I got discouraged about my athletic ability, I would break out that old yearbook and read Coach Adams' words to me. They became my passion fuel.

What applies to sports, applies to telling others about Jesus, as well. Passion fuel can overcome any inability, disability, or excuse. Passion fuel can give you the internal thrust to bust through the perceived barriers that are keeping you from sharing your faith in Jesus.

What are those roadblocks for you?

Maybe you don't know how to share your faith. Don't worry, passion fuel will motivate you to discover how (and reading and applying this book will help too!).

Maybe you are afraid of what your friends will think if you start sharing Jesus with them. Passion fuel will give you the internal motivation to run that fear right over and to share Jesus in spite of the quiver in your voice and knocking in your knees.

Perhaps you are not living a life that backs up your message. You are kind of afraid that if you start sharing Jesus with your friends that they will point out this inconsistency. Passion fuel will give you the strength to start living differently so that what comes out of your life and your lips are not contradicting each other.

Whatever your roadblock, passion fuel will help you drive right through it!

Just as there are different kinds of foods you can use to fuel your physical body, there are several different kinds of passion fuel that can fuel you spiritually, when sharing your faith. Let's take a look at four of the most common. These aren't the only kinds of passion fuel, but they are right at the top of the list for getting your heart pulsing and your energy focused!

1 OBEDIENCE TO GOD

For some believers, their primary motivation for sharing their faith is simple obedience to God. "God told me to in the Bible, so I'll do it." When they read Jesus' command in Matthew 28:19 "Go and make disciples…" they see it as their prime directive. So they set about to make sharing God's message a priority in their lives.

There's a lot to be said for doing something simply because God told us we're supposed to! The Bible also stirs in another spiritual reality that can sober us and further engage our passion to obey God by sharing our faith: a healthy, respectful fear of God. In 2 Corinthians 5:10-11, one of the greatest evangelists of all time, the apostle Paul, described how his fear of God motivated him to share Jesus' message:

> For we must all appear before the judgment seat of Christ, that each one may receive what is due him for the things done while in the body, whether good or bad. Since, then, we know what it is to fear the Lord, we try to persuade men.

If we take a long, hard look at Jesus' clear directive to "go and make disciples," simple obedience should actually be all the motivation any of us needs. But God graciously provides us with other passion fuels that can help stir us to action if there are times when simple obedience isn't enough to hold our focus.

② LOVE FOR GOD

Our love for God and God's love for us is a powerful type of passion fuel. When Jesus has done so much for us, we can feel compelled to serve Him out of a deep love and that includes sharing His marvelous message with others. When He's become everything to us, we want to share this relationship that has so profoundly changed our lives.

Really, it's like anything else we're passionate about. If we spend time with someone, before long they're going to hear about the things we love. Like for me, if you hang with me, it won't be long before you'll hear about my wife, my kids, my favorite sports team, and so on. We talk with our friends about that which we love. And if we love God deeply, we talk about Him.

The apostle Paul describes it this way in 2 Corinthians 5:14, 18-20:

> For Christ's love compels us, because we are convinced that one died for all, and therefore all died...All this is from God, who reconciled us to himself through Christ and gave us the ministry of reconciliation: that God was reconciling the world to himself in Christ, not counting men's sins against them. And he has committed to us the message of reconciliation. We are therefore Christ's ambassadors, as though God were making his appeal through us. We implore you on Christ's behalf: Be reconciled to God.

So this same apostle Paul who described for us earlier how his fear of God motivated him to share Jesus is now describing, just a few verses later, how Christ's love compels him, as well. How can love of God and fear of God go together in the same breath? At first glance it does seem like a contradiction, but if you think about it, it's actually quite possible to love and fear something at the same time.

The ocean is a concrete example of something that can stir both love and fear simultaneously. I may love the ocean with its majesty and grandeur, but I also have a healthy respect and, yes, outright fear of it because its immense power can be unleashed through its mighty waves. In the same way, it's possible to love and fear God at the same time.

3 YOUR FRIENDS NEED JESUS NOW!

Whether they know it or not, your friends need Jesus right now. We humans were made with an invisible, unquenchable need for God. Life without God is like having a car without an engine, a cell phone without a service provider, or a book without words. It's the existence of God that gives us the basis for hope. It's the love of God that gives us the reason to hope.

If there is a God who loved us enough to send His Son to die for our sins, then life is worth living. Why? Because if this God exists then everything we do on this earth matters for eternity!

Can you imagine living a life without the hope of Jesus? Sure, there are some temporary fun fixes—drugs, sexual promiscuity, drinking, and partying, just to name a few. And, yes, there are some "non-sin" pastimes that one can enjoy apart from Jesus—such as friends, sports, hobbies, clothes and family.

But apart from God, at the core of every human is a gaping hole. This hole can be temporarily filled with friends, sports, or sin. But it doesn't stick. Some who recognize this keep trying harder and harder to fill that hole. They try to pack it with more and more escape activities. But no matter how much stuff they stuff into it, it is never fully filled. Why? Because the hole is too big for anything on this side of eternity! The only thing that can truly, fully, and permanently fill that gaping hole is a relationship with Jesus Christ.

TRUE CONFESSIONS

In the midst of our busy schedules, we can sometimes get side-tracked from seeing the hurt around us. Let me tell you about one heartbreaking incident where this happened to me.

Pat was the shift manager of the restaurant where I used to prepare sermons when I was a pastor. I saw her almost every morning. We talked politely. She knew I was a pastor and I knew that she knew. I kept thinking that I would bring the gospel up later. Later never came. One day I came into the restaurant and Pat wasn't there to greet me. So I seated myself in my normal booth and began to study. Sarah, the waitress who worked the same shift as Pat, began pouring coffee in my cup as my head was buried in my Bible. I noticed her hand was trembling as she poured the coffee. Looking up I noticed a tear streaming down her cheek. I asked what was wrong. "Oh, haven't you heard?" she sobbed. "Last night Pat killed herself."

I was stunned. Pat seemed like an intelligent, mentally stable middle-aged lady. But underneath her smiling façade a cauldron of worthless feelings had been stirred by the finger of the devil. A tear came streaming down my cheek at that moment. Not just because I lost a friend, but because I missed an opportunity, countless opportunities, to tell her about Jesus.

I was too busy preparing sermons.

Never again.

From the outside looking in, your friends who don't know Jesus may look happy and fulfilled. They may seem like they have true joy and purpose on this earth. But if you could see into the secret chambers of their soul you would see this black hole of secret longing that can only be filled and fulfilled by Jesus.

When Jesus walked the earth He could see this cold, dark rift in the souls of people. Here's what the Bible says about Jesus' ability to see into the souls of those around Him: "When he saw the crowds, he had compassion on them, because they were harassed and helpless, like sheep without a shepherd" (Matthew 9:36). Thousands of people were following Jesus and He could see that black hole of hopelessness in their souls. He felt sorry for them. He hurt for them.

Do you hurt for your friends who don't know Jesus? And not just them; what about the crowds of students at your school? Look at them through the eyes of Jesus and let your compassion for the lost become your passion fuel. Imagine that gaping hole in their souls and then be willing to do whatever it takes to fill it with Jesus.

4 ETERNAL REALITIES

For some Christians, the eternal realities of heaven and hell serve as a driving passion fuel for sharing their faith. William Booth, founder of The Salvation Army, once said that he wished he could take his leaders and dangle them over the flames of hell explaining "If they could see the flames and smell the smoke and feel the heat and hear the cries of the damned, they would go out to preach what they had seen and heard. They would then preach like dying men to dying people."[1]

If you could take 10 Christian leaders and let them see the horrors of hell for 24 hours, I believe that those leaders would shake the world for Jesus when they got back to earth. But I am equally convinced that if you could take just one Christian man, woman, boy, or girl and let him/her see the glory of God for 24 seconds, this person would single-handedly reach the world with the gospel.

Why do I say that? Because it kind of already happened! Check out the words of the apostle Paul in 2 Corinthians 12:2-4 (hint: "the man" Paul is talking about here is himself):

> I know a man in Christ who fourteen years ago was caught up to the third heaven. Whether it was in the body or out of the body I do not know—God knows. And I know that this man—whether in the body or apart from the body I do not know, but God knows—was caught up to paradise. He heard inexpressible things, things that man is not permitted to tell.

If there was ever one man who single-handedly shook the world for God, it was the apostle Paul. What motivated him? It sure seems that his primary motivation (AKA "passion fuel") came from what he saw in heaven. Whatever it was, it blew him away and gave him a glimpse of what is to come for every believer in Jesus.[2]

Clearly, heaven can be a strong motivation for sharing our faith. But what about hell—the more disturbing of the two eternal realities?

I have a confession to make that may surprise you. I have a serious problem with the doctrine of hell. It's hard to imagine a loving God who would create an eternal place of suffering for sinners. Don't get me wrong; I think that sinners should suffer some. But an eternity of agony in "fire and brimstone" for all those who happen not to be Christians? Come on!

It's a lot easier to imagine hell as a place where people are not physically tortured but psychologically tormented until

CAN I GET A WITNESS?

My name is Chelsi! I am 16 years old and I live in Fairborn, Ohio! I attended a Dare 2 Share conference and wasn't expecting my life to change as much as it did in a matter of two days! I watched the drama "Letter from Hell" and I took the 48-hour challenge [to share my faith with a friend within 48 hours]. Honestly I thought it would be the hardest thing to do, but when I walked into school on Monday I looked at people as if they were burning in hell! I could not stand it. I could not believe I was letting my friends go to hell! From that weekend on, I opened a conversation up about God and His Son Jesus Christ every chance I could get! Many people have given their hearts to the Lord this year, and it wouldn't have happened if I hadn't told them the GOSPEL!

they regret and repent. Maybe at this point they are even given a second chance to respond to Christ. This kind of hell seems to have the best of both worlds: Sinners are punished and then mercy is demonstrated. Perhaps the exception to this rule is the worst of the worst sinners. Those who commit mass murder in the name of some warped ideology like Hitler and Stalin could burn forever as far as I'm concerned.

Or maybe hell could be mere annihilation—eternal extinction of the soul, if you will. When people are plunged into that infernal inferno, it is a final purging of existence. Their slates are wiped clean and they cease to be. As horrible as that may sound, it is infinitely more fathomable than an *eternal* hell.

I have a problem with accepting a doctrine that condemns the sinner to a forever future without hope, without escape, without a second chance. To be honest my heart begins to hurt and my brain starts to ache when I think about it. Questions flood my mind and challenge my convictions. Questions like how could a loving God send people to an eternity in fire and brimstone? And if God is so merciful why would He cause people to suffer for so long in such pain?

But no matter how many times I try to explain hell away or redefine and make it palatable to my puny brain, there it is in black and white again and again throughout the pages of the Bible. No matter how I try to imagine it away or tone it down, one thing is clear: The Bible describes hell as for real and forever.

Jesus throws kerosene on the flames when He speaks so matter-of-factly about a literal hell. Did you know that the Son of God spoke more about hell than heaven? Of the 12 times that hell (*gehenna*, in the original Greek) is mentioned in the New Testament, 11 are mentioned by Jesus. And He never described hell as figurative, temporary, or anything less than horrific. Five different times He calls it a place of "weeping and gnashing of teeth." I'm not even sure what gnashing of teeth is, but it doesn't sound pleasant.

Speaking of unpleasant thoughts, check out these verses about hell:

> He will punish those who do not know God and do not obey the gospel of our Lord Jesus. They will be punished with everlasting destruction and shut out from the presence of the Lord and from the majesty of his power. (2 Thessalonians 1:8-9)

> "[Anyone who worships evil] will drink of the wine of God's fury, which has been poured full strength into the cup of his wrath. He will be tormented with burning sulfur in the presence of the holy angels and of the Lamb. And the smoke

of their torment rises for ever and ever. There is no rest day or night." (Revelation 14:10-11)

The list of verses goes on and on and on. From the Old Testament to the New Testament, from prophets to the apostles to Jesus Himself, hell is described with real and raw adjectives as your worst fears come true and then multiplied by infinity for eternity.

Here is where the troubling question rears its ugly head once again. How could a loving God send people whom He created to suffer in an eternal hell?

And maybe that question is the problem. Oftentimes the twenty-first century version of the Christian God is *just* loving instead of *just* and *loving*. The just part of God (that demands absolute justice, holiness, and perfection) has been minimized and the loving part of God (that shows mercy, grace, and forgiveness) has been maximized. As a result, we have tailored our view into a God who is big on love and light on bite. He becomes more of a cosmic Santa Claus who caters to our every whim, rather than the King of Kings and Lord of Lords.

While most of us Christians believe in some kind of hell, we usually just don't bring it up much. It is an unpleasant subject and leads to too many questions about the character of God. Hell is that crazy doctrine that we keep locked in the basement of our belief systems. We all know that it is there, chained to the underbelly of the theology of the holiness of God. We hope that it stays in the shadows and never comes up in conversation. Why? Because if people found out what we really believed they would think we were radicals, extremists, and kooks. If hell isn't real, then maybe we are.

But if it is real, then why aren't we more intense, more aggressive, more intentional, more urgent? If hell is real (and the Bible says it is) then we should be motivated to keep as many people as we can out of it—friends, foes, teachers, classmates, coworkers, teammates, family members, strangers. . . everybody.

WHAT GETS YOU REVED?

Which kind of passion fuel revs you up and gets your motivational motor running as you live THE Cause out loud? Maybe you are more driven out of your love for Jesus or you want to share Christ because He told you to! If it's compassion for your friends now or fear of hell for them later, then go for it!

As you unlock what gets you in gear, slowly start adding other types of fuel into your mix. Passion fuels are often better together. Paul, that greatest of all evangelist, describes being motivated by all of them throughout his ministry. And Jesus used all of them to motivate his disciples to live THE Cause. Mixing in new passion fuels can give us a fresh perspective on the priority sharing our faith should play in our lives.

Use your imagination as you tap into your passion fuels. As you add "love for God," imagine a heavenly embrace from your father. When your fuel is "compassion for the lost," visualize the pain of a life without Jesus. If you're adding "obedience to God," imagine a father who's smiling. Or visualize the judgment seat or the reality of heaven or hell.

But regardless of the passion fuel mix that's right for you, it's critical that you ignite your human motivation into action through the power of the Holy Spirit! For when we depend on the Holy Spirit we have divine power to evangelize that goes far beyond our own human motivations and powers of persuasion. While it's your job to be faithful to Christ's call to participate in His search and rescue mission, it's the Spirit's job to move hearts and souls and call them "out of darkness and into His wonderful light" (1 Peter 2:9).

So fuel up! Passion fuel will help you stay focused and purposeful in the midst of the ups and downs of your faith-sharing journey.

FIRESTARTER

I recently wrote a fiction book that relates what can happen when just one teen is passionate about Jesus' mission to reach the lost. If you're looking for a power boost for your faith-sharing passion, pick up a copy of *Firestarter* at www.dare2share.org/store. As you follow the sparks that fly when the message of the gospel spreads across one high school campus, you'll be challenged to share your faith with your friends and reach your own school with Jesus' message!

chapter 3

HOW TO OVERCOME YOUR FEARS

What will my friends think if I talk about Jesus? Will they reject me? What if they ask me some question I don't know how to answer? They know I'm not perfect, will they think I'm a hypocrite if I start talking about God?

Let's be honest. Most all of us wrestle with these kinds of fears when we think about sharing our faith with others. But did you know that God has provided us with an incredibly powerful resource that can help us overcome our fears? It's called prayer.

No matter what your fears, prayer will help you face them down. Because prayer is the way you tap into the power of the Holy Spirit who will give you courage, insight and strength. Prayer is how you lay the groundwork for the spiritual battle you're entering into for the souls of your friends.

What does prayer look like when it comes to reaching your friends who need Jesus? It looks like you praising God for who He is, what He's done and what He's going to do. It looks like you taking your fears to Him and humbly asking for the courage, strength and wisdom you need to reach out and share His message. It looks like you storming the throne room of heaven on behalf of the souls of your friends. Let's take a look at how prayer can help you face down three of the most common faith-sharing fears.

MY FRIENDS MIGHT REJECT ME

Fear of rejection seems to be the biggest fear most of us wrestle with when we start down the road of sharing our faith with our friends. And not without good reason. The Bible and church history are stacked and packed with the stories of those who suffered rejection and persecution for their faith—starting with Jesus Himself and His inner circle of hand-picked followers, most of whom were martyred for their faith. But before visions of being fed to the lions begin to haunt your dreams, take heart, because the same something that made Jesus' early followers strong and courageous is available to you too!

What was it that compelled them to stand firm and spread Jesus' message in the face of such fearsome consequences? How did they do it? By tapping into the very presence of God through prayer.

What does that mean? Imagine an electrical outlet right in the middle of your chest. That outlet is the Spirit of God. If you choose to plug into Him through prayer, He will give you a sustained current of spiritual power to share the gospel with anybody you encounter and live a life that supports the message you are sharing. But you have to plug into His power through faith and prayer.

The apostle Paul wrote these words to the Christians who lived in Ephesus: "I pray that out of his glorious riches he may strengthen you with *power through his Spirit in your inner being*" (Ephesians 3:16). Notice that this is not just strength. It is mighty inner strength that God provides through His Holy Spirit.

Just like the great Apostle Paul, who you could safely say had plenty of experience on the faith-sharing front, we need to tap into God's power and pray for boldness when sharing the gospel. In Ephesians 6:19 we see Paul recruiting others to pray alongside him: "Pray also for me, that whenever I speak, words may be given me so that I will fearlessly make known the mystery of the gospel."

So pray, pray, pray! Then step out on the firm conviction that God goes with you as you reach out to your friends. As soon as you ask for His strength He will meet you in your need. Although you may not feel some spiritual sensation reverberating and you may still feel awkward or uncomfortable, the Spirit is there nonetheless. He will help you overcome your fears and empower you to live and share your faith.

I love Acts 4:31. Here Luke, the author of Acts, writes, "After they prayed, the place where they were meeting was shaken. And they were all filled with the Holy Spirit and spoke the word of

CAN I GET A WITNESS?

My name is Madelyn. I'm 13 and from St. Louis, Missouri. After I went to a Dare 2 Share conference last year I really wanted to witness to my dad but did not have the strength to do it on my own. I realized that I need the Holy Spirit to guide me and to give me the courage to lead him to Christ. All through the Bible there are stories of how the Holy Spirit can do amazing things if we just let Him. Witnessing to my dad was a mountain in my journey, but with the Holy Spirit inside of me it's only a bump in the road.

God boldly." Notice that the building is shaken with the power of prayer, then the believers are shaken with the power of the Spirit and, finally, the city is shaken with the power of the gospel. Suffice it to say, there's a whole lot of shaking going on. And it all started with prayer. If you want to reach your friends for Christ, if you want to make an impact at your school you need to start by shaking things up through prayer! When you do, the Spirit will shake you up and, as a result, you'll shake your friends up through your bold and loving declaration of the good news of Jesus through your life and your lips.

I WON'T KNOW WHAT TO SAY

Another common faith-sharing fear that prayer can help us face down is the fear of not knowing what to say if we get asked questions about God. There's no denying that the prospect of trying to explain God to others is a big job. After all, God is so immense that our puny brains are easily overwhelmed trying to comprehend Him. But that's one of the marvels of God's plan in sending us Jesus.

Jesus is God brought down to earth so that we humans can catch a glimpse of what God's like. It's Jesus who enables us to step into a personal and powerful relationship with the God of the universe and begin to comprehend Him. And we get to know Jesus better by spending time with Him in prayer and in His Word.

As we set out to share Jesus' message, the closer our relationship with Him, the better we will be able to introduce our friends to Him. When our faith-sharing efforts are bathed in prayer, we can rest in the knowledge that God goes with us and will guide us.

But even if we're tight with Jesus and are spending time in prayer and in His Word, there will be times when we don't know the answers to the questions that might come our way. When that happens—and it will—just remember that it's always OK to respond to someone's inquires with an honest, "I don't know, but I'll do my best to find out. Let's meet again soon."

Here's how it works. Say somebody asks you a question about your faith that you don't know how to answer. Simply respond with the "I'll find out" statement. Then prayerfully go back to your Bible, youth leader, or pastor to find an answer. You can also surf around www.dare2share.org or gotquestions.org to try to find the answer to your question.

Not only does this approach give you time to find an answer, it also uses three little words that every Christian should learn: "I don't know!" It shows a bit of humility that is greatly needed in many Christian circles today. Too many times Christians act like know-it-alls about all things eternal. Sure, there is a lot that we can know, a lot of stuff that is crystal clear from the Word of God. We can stand on that in humble confidence. But there is a lot we don't know and some stuff we can't know for sure. Maybe that's why Paul the apostle (who knew a lot of stuff) made it clear that there are many things we can't know on this side of eternity. Listen to his words in 1 Corinthians 13:12: "Now we see but a poor reflection as in a mirror; then we shall see face to face. Now I know in part; then I shall know fully, even as I am fully known."

Only when we are in heaven will we be able to be 100 percent sure about everything. Until then, we stand on the truths that we can know and we seek God's wisdom to begin the never-ending journey of learning more from God's Word and Spirit.

TRUE CONFESSIONS

When I was in high school I failed miserably at this. As I already stated, I wasn't competitive in sports due to an almost clinical lack of physical coordination. But I was, I'm sad to say, extremely competitive in all things spiritual, including sharing my faith. I hated not having the answers. There were times I so wanted to win the argument I'd make up facts (that's called lying) if need be, to convince them I was right. Two things happened as a result: 90 percent of the time they rejected Christ anyway. The old saying is right, "You can't argue somebody into the kingdom." And I lost my spiritual reward for those faith-sharing attempts. Even spiritual acts like sharing your faith don't get rewarded when done out of competitiveness or used with deceit. I thank the Lord that this was just a short fleshly phase in my life, and God taught me how to be honest when I didn't have the answer.

Believe it or not, the humility that is shown in not having all the answers on the spot may very well open the door for your friend to be receptive to hearing the gospel. Why? Because in a world drenched in arrogance, this kind of humility may be a stronger argument for the genuineness of Christianity than the best arguments in the world.

Another benefit of using this statement is that it helps you learn more about your faith. The bottom line is that most of us aren't going to take a "How to Share the Gospel with Anyone from Any Cult, Philosophy, or World Religion" class that covers everything. Even if we did, there would be a lot that we would forget or not get. But when you learn one conversation at a time, you tend not to forget those lessons. When you keep saying, "That's a great question! I don't know, but I'll find out. Let's meet again soon," you create a lifestyle of study and learning that goes deeper into your brain. And it gives you time to pray specifically for your friends and the issues they're wrestling with as they consider Jesus and His message! Another plus is that unresolved questions are actually a great opportunity to reopen the conversation and get others thinking about God again!

So don't let the fear of not having all the answers keep you down. Pray, be humble, pray some more, do your research and follow up.

I'M NOT A PERFECT CHRISTIAN

Do you sometimes feel like you need to be a "perfect" Christian before you try to talk about Jesus with others? Are you worried that you'll seem hypocritical if your conversation gets all God-focused when your own walk with Jesus is still filled with ongoing everyday challenges like lying or lust. You're not alone if you sometimes fear that people will label you a judgmental hypocrite if you open your mouth to talk about God.

Again, prayer is the key to helping you move past this fear. When you take your sin struggles to God in prayer, you'll discover God's grace and forgiveness and His strength for getting back up after you fall. You'll find renewed determination to become more like Jesus. But you should always see your sin struggles as motivation to move your life toward Jesus, not as an excuse to avoid talking about Him with others!

The Bible even promises that the gospel can shine through you despite your weaknesses and imperfections. It says: "We now have this light shining in our hearts, but we ourselves are like fragile clay jars containing this great treasure. This makes it clear that our great power is from God, not from ourselves" (2 Corinthians 4:7, NLT).

Our lives in Christ may be chipped and cracked and far from perfect, but God can still communicate His message of grace through us. In fact in many ways, sharing the gospel with others out of your own brokenness and spiritual struggle allows you to declare God's grace to a hurting world more authentically than any prim, proper, polished, plastic preacher ever could. I'd even go so far as to say that your friends aren't looking for a "perfect" Christian, they're looking for a "real" one.

Your struggles and stumbles keep you humble and real. And it's in your humility that God can really unleash His power and perfection. Maybe you've heard the old saying that goes: "Evangelism is just one beggar showing another where to find food." So don't worry about waiting until you manage to get all spiffed up and decked out in your cleanest, finest spiritual duds. Just humbly confess your sin to God in prayer and then step out and offer Jesus to your friends regardless of your imperfect appearance on the outside. Pass this news that's too good to keep to yourself along!

PRAYER IS YOUR PRIMARY FEAR-BUSTER

Prayer is definitely your starting and ending point for overcoming your faith-sharing fears. Always remember that sharing Jesus' message takes you into the spiritual realm where, when all is said and done, your friends are impacted not by smooth talk or great debating skills, but by the power of the Holy Spirit touching their hearts and souls.

That's why prayer is central.

So plug into the power of the Holy Spirit through prayer, ask God to prepare the hearts of your friends and then move out into the spiritual battle with courage and conviction. Since sharing the gospel is the most eternally impacting thing you'll ever do, it's no wonder the prospect of talking about Jesus with others can sometimes make you quiver in your boots. Just take your fears to God in prayer and watch Him help you face them down.

Don't throw dirt clods at Satan. Bust out the bazooka of prayer hidden in your closet. That will put him on the run. Say hello to my little friend...called prayer.

chapter 4

HOW TO SHARE JESUS IN A RELATIONAL AND RELENTLESS WAY

For the most part, we live in a diverse, live-and-let-live culture where an attitude of tolerance and acceptance of varying religious beliefs is highly valued. Don't get me wrong, tolerance and acceptance are good things—we should never set ourselves up as judge and jury over someone else's soul, since that is definitely in God's job description and not ours.

But sometimes I think we get confused about what it means to be tolerant and accepting. In fact, sometimes I think we shy away from initiating spiritual conversations with our friends because we're concerned that just talking about Jesus will come across as intrusive or intolerant.

But nothing could be further from the truth! I can be tolerant and accepting of someone, but still believe they are desperately wrong and in need of help.

Take a concrete example from the physical world. Say I believe in gravity, but you don't—you've never seen it, so you've concluded that it's just some fabricated conspiracy to keep people down. I can be tolerant of you as a person, accepting you for who you are, but still hold the very strong conviction that you are wrong in your belief that gravity doesn't exist. Then one day you decide you're going to jump off a cliff. I fear for you and feel compassion for you, even as you are blind to a truth that seems clear to me. Out of love and concern I can try to do everything in my power to convince you that gravity is real. But you jump anyway, and SPLAT, it's over for you.

Was I bigoted or judgmental because I tried to communicate the truth to you? No, I was expressing my care and concern for you. The same is true when it comes to the spiritual realm. If I believe there are spiritual realities that you need to understand and be warned about, I would be doing you a great disservice if I failed to share what I know with you.

BALANCING RELATIONAL AND RELENTLESS EVANGELISM

That's the beauty of relational evangelism! What exactly do I mean by that term "relational evangelism"? I mean sharing Jesus' message with a loving, listening patience across your network of relationships: friends—both real world and online, classmates, teammates, co-workers, family, neighbors and so on.

Because you care about these people God has placed in your life, you won't come across as a judgmental know-it-all when you bring Jesus up in conversation. Right out of the starting block, when you share your faith with those you know personally, you are already several strides ahead in terms of impact! Friend's hold way more influence over other friends than any stranger ever could—as I mentioned earlier, one study shows that a friend has one hundred times more influence than a stranger.[1] Why?

Because "people don't care how much you know, until they know how much you care."

Relational evangelism moves spiritual discussions out of the realm of a debate of ideas between strangers. It helps you reduce the likelihood that you'll come across as an argumentative, haughty Christian itching to win debating points rather than a genuine friend striving to reach into others' lives with Jesus' love and message of grace. Have you ever met anyone who's been successfully argued into the Kingdom of God? It just doesn't happen. That's one of the things that makes relational evangelism so much more impacting!

Another strength of relational evangelism is that you will be far more loving, listening and patient than any stranger ever would be. And you know your friends—their struggles, their issues, their story, their lives. Knowing them can help you explain the gospel in a way that is more likely to reach into their hearts and impact their souls. I call this "Soul Apologetics" and you'll be learning more about it in Chapter 18.

Relational evangelism is powerful, but as the title of this chapter indicates, there's another dimension to effective sharing. You must learn to be relentless as well! You must always guard against the temptation to just sit back and let your friends simply observe your life and wait for them to ask you question about Jesus. Because there's an urgency and authority to the gospel that also requires that you bring a relentless determination to share Jesus' message to your friends. That's why sharing your faith must be both relational *and* relentless!

What does relentless evangelism look like? It speaks, it confronts and it's persistent. And I'll tell you what it doesn't look like. Relentless evangelism isn't about arguing, badgering or belittling. Instead, it's a dogged persistence that doesn't give up on your friends—a determination that keeps on loving them and sharing with them through months and years.

Not everyone is ready to trust in Jesus the first time they hear the gospel. While some may be on the short road to Jesus, others have a longer road to travel before His truth connects in their soul. And sadly, for some, it may never connect. But only God knows who falls into which category! So our job is to do our best to doggedly pursue and persuade our friends to consider Jesus' message.

OUR DRIVE COMES FROM JESUS HIMSELF

Where does this relentless drive to continue to share Jesus with our lost friends come from? It comes from Jesus Himself.

Just before Jesus ascended into heaven He told His disciples: "All authority in heaven and on earth has been given to me. Therefore go and make disciples of all nations, baptizing them in the name of the Father and of the Son and of the Holy Spirit, and teaching them to obey everything I have commanded you. And surely I am with you always, to the very end of the age" (Matthew 28:18-20). Basically Jesus is telling His disciples (and if you are a follower of Jesus then you are a disciple, too) that we have the right, responsibility, and reason to relationally and relentlessly share the message of Jesus.

We have the right to share this message because Jesus has the authority and has authorized us to go and make disciples out of everybody on this planet! Even in parts of the world where sharing the gospel is illegal we have the right to share our faith. Why? Because the Son of God Himself gave us the right!

We have the responsibility to share this message because Jesus commanded us to do it! This passage of Scripture that we now call "THE Cause" was originally nicknamed "The Great Commission," not "The Good Suggestion," for a reason. It is not optional. God Himself is telling us to go and share this message with everybody we can. We can walk in confidence, knowing that when we share Jesus with others in a loving, caring way, we are living out God's call on our lives to make disciples.

We have the reason to share this message because Jesus goes with us! He tells us that He is with us always, even to the end of the age. Stop and think about that for a moment. The God of the universe is with you every second of every day. Jesus is with you at school, when you drive down the street, when you are over at your friend's house, when you are surfing the Internet, and when you are playing sports. He is with you every day and all the time.

If you could see Him would you be embarrassed to introduce Him to your friends? No way! You'd go up to your friends and say, "Hey, I want to introduce you to my best friend, Jesus. Have you two ever met?" If you could see Jesus you would never be embarrassed to introduce Him to your friends. Okay, brace yourself; this is where it gets a little convicting.

The Bible tells us in 2 Corinthians 5:7 that we should "live by faith, not by sight." In other words, we should live as though we can see the invisible. We should walk by what we know to be true

WARNING!

Remember! Although we have the right to relentlessly share our faith, we need to make sure that we do it with love and humility. Otherwise, nobody is going to want to hear about it!

and not just by what we can see with the human eye. How does all this apply to you and sharing the gospel with your friends? Simple: If Jesus tells us that He is with us to the end of the age, then He is with us. We should live like He is right at our side all the time and talk about Him with boldness.

MY COUSIN ERIC

I don't come from a typical religious, Bible-reading, church-going family. I come from a family of bodybuilding, tobacco-chewing, beer-drinking thugs. Many of my cousins and uncles are title-winning bodybuilders. I don't know what happened to me. I got ripped off by the gene pool.

One of my cousins, Eric, is especially big. At one point he could bench-press well above the 500-pound mark. He is 5' 8" tall and about 5' 8" wide. Suffice it to say that he is huge.

Once when I was in high school I was talking to two teenage boys who were especially negative to the message of the gospel. As I started sharing with them about Jesus, they began making fun of me. That was a mistake, a big one.

Eric, who is a believer, was leaning against a wall about 10 feet away, listening in to our conversation. When these two guys started making fun of his scrawny little cousin (that would be me), he slowly lumbered his gigantic frame over to the snickering teens. With pecs flexed and biceps bulging he glared into their eyes and said, "This is my cousin. If you don't listen to what he has got to say you are going to want to know where you will go when you die . . . because you will die."

Suddenly these two poor teenagers were downright "interested" in the gospel message. They smiled and nodded and said they would trust in Christ right away. Trembling and terrified they prayed with me right there. I don't know if they really became Christians or were just going through the motions because my cousin was standing by my side. All I do know is that I sure liked having Eric right there next to me while I was talking about Jesus. I thought to myself, *If I could just take my cousin Eric with me wherever I went sharing, I would never be afraid again. If someone wouldn't trust in Christ I could just say, "Eric, beat the sin out of them."* Just kidding. I would never do that. But the whole incident made me think about a person and a presence bigger than Eric.

I suddenly realized that the maker of heaven and earth (and Eric) dwells inside of me and goes with me everywhere I go ... Jesus Christ Himself. When I'm afraid to share my faith I try to reflect on that promise of Jesus' presence, and I am suddenly infused with a new sense of confidence. "I am with you always" ... always.

He is always there to encourage, coach, strengthen, and enable us. He is always with us. This mind-blowing truth frees us from the crushing burden of feeling like it's our fault if our friends don't respond to the gospel—for not everyone who hears the gospel will trust in Jesus, as the Parable of the Sower in Matthew 13 makes clear. Still it is our responsibility to share, while it is God's responsibility to save and it is our friends' responsibility to respond.

FINDING THE BALANCE

Relational and relentless. Both are important. So balance is what we need. Relational evangelism loves, listens and is patient.

Relentless evangelism confronts, speaks and is persistent. It's a bit like a teeter totter, sometimes one side's up while the other is down, but then they can switch and be opposite. Just keep working to find that balance between relational **and** relentless sharing, knowing that God is always with you and has called you to THE Cause of causes.

HOW TO KNOW THE TRUTH

I'll never forget the conversation in the McDonald's that day. It went something like this:

Guy: "How do you know there's truth?"

Me: "We all exist on the basis of certain truths. We don't jump off of tall buildings because of the truth about gravity. We do fly in airplanes because of the truth about aerodynamics. There are truths in relationships like forgiveness, honesty, and loyalty that work. There are truths in everything. We exist by truth."

Guy: "How do we know that we are not the figment of somebody else's imagination? How do you even know you're even right here? How do I know I'm really here?"

Me: "Let me pour your hot coffee in your lap and you'll know you're here."

We talked for a while longer. He didn't trust in Christ as his Savior right on the spot, but our conversation made him take a second look at Jesus and the claims of Christ.

My conversation that day represents the kind of philosophical conflict you may be facing with your non-Christian friends. The comment I most often get from teenagers goes something like, "Well, that's true for you. My truth is a little different."

Really?

Like we talked about briefly in the previous chapter, you can't get away from truth. If you take a flying leap off the Empire State Building, I'll be waiting at the bottom with a scooper and a body bag!

Truth is truth. It's not dependent on your perspective or acceptance of it. Truth is truth with or without you.

Truth is not a popularity contest. If 99 out of 100 people believe that black is white and up is down, up does not become down and white does not become black.

The same is true with spiritual truth. If Jesus is God then Allah is not, Joseph Smith was wrong, and Buddha is in trouble. If Jesus is not God then He was a kook. Why? Because He claimed to be God! He told His disciples in John 10:30, "I and the Father are one." In other words, Jesus Christ is every bit as much God as the heavenly Father is!

Not only that, but Jesus claimed to be the only way to get to heaven. Listen to His words in John 14:6: "I am the way and the truth and the life. No one comes to the Father except through me."

Notice the word that Jesus uses and which one He doesn't. He claims to be *the* way, not *a* way; *the* truth, not *a* truth; *the* life, not *a* life.

The whole "well, that's true for you" argument doesn't fly with Jesus. He is the Author of truth and what He speaks is truth.

TRUTH, PROOF AND FAITH

If there is truth can we know it for sure? What about proof? Can I really prove my Christianity? Where does faith come in?

All of these are great and relevant questions, especially in a culture where we are encouraged to each have our own customized versions of personal truth. And while nobody except God Himself knows all truth, there are some spiritual truths that we can know for sure.

The key word here is "enough." He gives us enough proof so that we can respond in faith and believe Him. In legal language it's called "a preponderance of evidence." Basically, this means that what a jury needs is enough evidence to convict or acquit somebody. They don't need more or less, just enough.

God gives us enough evidence in areas we can test Him in (such as fulfilled prophecies, and archaeological, historical, and scientific evidences of the Bible's validity) to trust Him in the areas we can't test Him in (heaven, hell, spiritual truth in the invisible realm). In this preponderance of evidence we have all we need to believe.

If you have a friend who says, "I want proof that God is there!" you can show him the creation, evidence of His existence. You can show him hundreds of fulfilled prophecies from the Old Testament. You can demonstrate the reliability of the Bible in all areas.

But let's say he says, "Well, if God is real then why doesn't He come down right now and prove it?" What do you do then? You can tell him two things. The first is that He did just that once when Jesus became the God-man. The second is that if He "came down" every time an unbeliever wanted proof, then where would faith come in?

God gives us enough evidence so that we can take the next step of faith in full confidence that He is there. But this step is not a leap into the darkness. It's a step into the light!

What does this mean for you?

Again, consider Jesus words in John 14:6: "I am the way and the truth and the life. No one comes to the Father except through me." Did you catch that? Jesus said He was "***the truth.***" When you take the step of putting your faith and trust in Jesus, you can have confidence that His words are truth. And since the Spirit of Jesus inspired the writers of the Bible, then you can take what they wrote in the Holy Scriptures as truth as well.

TRUTH WE CAN KNOW FROM GOD'S WORD

Does that mean that we can know all truth? No way! Our brains are too puny to hold it all. Only God knows all truth.

But we can know some truth. And the sum of the truth that we can know with confidence is what God's Word clearly states. For instance, here are four core truths that the Bible emphasizes again and again.

 GOD

You can know that there is a God, the Trinity if you will, one God in three: the Father, Son, and Holy Spirit. While we can't quite comprehend it, we accept it by faith. Here are a few verses that will help you: Deuteronomy 6:4, Isaiah 45:5, Matthew 3:16-17, Ephesians 4:4-6. This God is holy (hates sin)

and merciful (loves sinners), and always does what is right and just. He created everything in this universe and is holding it all together by the word of His power (Colossians 1:16-17). He sees everywhere, knows everything, and can do anything. He has always been here and will always be here. His name is "I AM" and because He is, we are!

2 JESUS, GOD'S SON

You can know that Jesus is God. He claimed to be God (John 10:28-30; 14:9), did miracles that could only be done by God (Matthew 8:23-27), and was recognized as God by those around Him (John 1:1, 14, 18). The ultimate proof that Jesus was God was His resurrection from the dead. He was seen by over 500 witnesses over the course of 40 days. If each of these witnesses testified in a court of law for 30 minutes, that would be 250 hours of testimony—that's 10 straight days of testimony. In the average court of law two or three solid witnesses are enough to convict or acquit. Jesus had more than 500 credible witnesses who were willing to risk their lives to say they had just seen Jesus. You can know that Jesus was and is God.

3 THE BIBLE

You can know that the Bible is God's Word, that it is fully trustworthy on every subject it refers to, from geography to archaeology to prophecy . . . anything that ends in a "y" (or any letter for that matter!). The Bible was written by 40 men over a period of 1,500 years. What are the chances that a group of guys, most of whom had never met each other, could write 66 books (that's how many "books" or sections are in the bigger book that we call "the Bible") without contradictions? The chances are zilch, unless God Himself oversaw, guided, and inspired the whole process. According to 2 Peter 1:20-21 and 2 Timothy 3:16-17, He did just that with the book that we call the Bible. This book itself is a miracle of God! It is packed full of fulfilled prophecies that are specific and spectacular!

(4) THE GOSPEL

You can know that Jesus died so you can have eternal life. The word gospel means "good news." It's the good news that Jesus died for our sins, rose again from the dead, and offers eternal life to all those who trust in Him alone for the forgiveness of their sins! The Bible makes it clear that God wants you to know that you have eternal life. Check this verse out in 1 John 5:13: "I write these things to you who believe in the name of the Son of God so that you may know that you have eternal life."

When you trust in Jesus alone you can know that you are in a personal, permanent relationship with the God of the universe, no doubt about it!

Why is it important you know that you can know these things? Because according to Hebrews 11:1, "Now faith is being sure of what we hope for and certain of what we do not see." In other words, if you can't be certain about some things then you can't have faith! Faith is being sure. It is being certain. It is being confident that what God says in His book is absolutely true!

Although you can't know everything, there are some things you can be absolutely certain are true. Among these truths are the existence of a personal and powerful God; the reliability of the Bible; that Jesus came, lived, died, and rose again; and that the gospel message is our means of eternal life!

These are truths we can bank our lives on! Does this mean we'll always have all the answers? No. There are some truths we can be sure of, and there are some that we really don't have a clue about! But God has given us a preponderance of evidence when it comes to these four core essentials of the Christian faith. Let's stand on what we know, share Jesus in humility with others, and continue to lean on God and learn more about Him as we grow in our walk with the Lord.

WARNING!

The temptation may be to think, *Isn't all this trusting in Jesus for salvation a little too easy?* But how easy is it to trust in a person you've never met (Jesus) to take you to a place you've never been (heaven)? How easy is it to stake your life and your eternal destiny on a man who lived 2,000 years ago and claimed to be God Himself? It's so easy that a child could do it and it's so hard that a self-righteous adult could choke on it. The reason that receiving the gift of eternal life is so simple and so "easy" is that Jesus did all the work for us. Maybe that's why He reminds us in Titus 3:5, "He saved us, not because of righteous things we had done, but because of his mercy. He saved us through the washing of rebirth and renewal by the Holy Spirit." It's not our hard work, but the hard work of Jesus, that saved us from sin. That's why it is so easy... Jesus did all the work! We simply receive it by faith!

CAN I GET A WITNESS?

My name is Kelcy. I am 15 years old and from Lincoln, Nebraska. It's by faith alone in Jesus alone that I'm forgiven—wow! For me, the idea that I have forgiveness just because of faith alone is such a hard concept to understand; yet completely mind-blowing. Here I am, a sinner, a rugged, unworthy sinner and because I made a decision to have faith that Jesus died for my sins, I get the amazing gift of forgiveness. It doesn't seem like it should be that simple— but the beauty of simplicity is what makes me fall in love with Jesus that much more."

chapter 6

HOW TO DISCOVER
YOUR SHARING STYLE

What do you think of when you hear the word *style*? If you are like most teenagers you probably think of clothes. Your style is mostly demonstrated by the types of clothes you wear. If you buy your clothes from Hollister you have one style. If you buy your clothes from Hot Topic you have a very different one.

Everybody's style is different and personal.

The same is true when it comes to sharing your faith. You have a specialized and supernaturally designed style of sharing that you must discover.

Your sharing style is determined through a combination of your personality, spiritual gifting, and emotional maturity. I believe that your style of sharing the gospel can change over the years as you continue to grow personally and spiritually.

DEBBIE AND ME

When I met Debbie I was blown away. She had the three G's that every spiritually oriented Christian guy is looking for: Good,

Godly, and Gorgeous! The more I got to know her, the more I was impressed. She loved God and loved others. The question was, would she love me? It took a while, but she finally came around.

After almost four years of dating we finally got married. Like many newlywed couples, we had a lot of conflict in our first few years of marriage. Some of these arguments came over our styles of sharing our faith.

You see, I had a pretty aggressive style of sharing Jesus. I loved to just bring Him up to others, especially teenagers. I found 12- to 18-year-olds especially open to talk about spiritual truths. From the time I was in junior high throughout much of my college years, I used to go to local shopping malls with my Christian friends and create conversations with teenagers about Jesus. More often than not I found teenagers were open to talk, share, debate, and sometimes believe!

Debbie didn't want to have anything to do with my style of evangelism. When she went to the mall she didn't think "sharing with the lost"; she thought "shop till you drop!"

We got into some arguments over the whole thing. She thought I was too pushy with my faith. I thought she was kind of wimpy about hers.

But then God taught me a lesson, a big one.

Debbie has been a fifth-grade public school teacher for years. In one school year, many years ago, she had the opportunity of leading 21 kids to Christ and brought five families out to our church! What is more, she never got one complaint, even from the anti-Christian parents. Why? For one, she did it all within the law (and mostly outside the classroom!). Another reason, the bigger reason, is that my wife may be the most loving, kind, and listening person you'll ever meet. Everybody, I mean everybody, loves her. Why? Because she cares about others and listens to them! She listens to them so much that when she talks about Jesus they listen to her!

After watching my wife's effectiveness as a follower of Jesus, I began to realize that there are different ways to share the message of Jesus. I began to do an intense study of the New Testament to discover the various styles of sharing one's faith. I discovered four. There may be more that I missed, but these four styles are the most obvious ways that the early Christians communicated the gospel message with others. Here are the styles that I discovered:

TALKERS, "STALKERS," BUDDIES AND BRAINS

Let's take a look at each of these four styles and the corresponding New Testament person who best represents that style. After we take a look at each of these four styles, we'll have you take a test to determine your own personal sharing style.

(1) TALKERS

Talkers are creative, funny, and easy to talk to. They are usually the life of the party and center of the conversation. They control the conversation, not by force but by sheer wit. When they share Jesus with others, they share the gospel in persuasive ways. What's their weakness? Because they are so people-centered and want to be liked, they sometimes can hold back because they are afraid to offend the person they are talking to at the moment.

Who is a biblical example of this style of sharing Jesus? Philip. Let me refresh your memory about this early follower of Jesus through this passage from the Bible that clearly shows his style of sharing Jesus:

Now an angel of the Lord said to Philip, "Go south to the road—the desert road—that goes down from Jerusalem to Gaza." So he started out, and on his way he met an Ethiopian eunuch, an important official in charge of all the treasury of Candace, queen of the Ethiopians. This man had gone to Jerusalem to worship, and on his way home was sitting in his chariot reading the book of Isaiah the prophet. The Spirit told Philip, "Go to that chariot and stay near it."

Then Philip ran up to the chariot and heard the man reading Isaiah the prophet. "Do you understand what you are reading?" Philip asked.

"How can I," he said, "unless someone explains it to me?" So he invited Philip to come up and sit with him.

The eunuch was reading this passage of Scripture:

"He was led like a sheep to the slaughter,
and as a lamb before the shearer is silent,
so he did not open his mouth.
In his humiliation he was deprived of justice.
Who can speak of his descendants?
For his life was taken from the earth."

The eunuch asked Philip, "Tell me, please, who is the prophet talking about, himself or someone else?" Then Philip began with that very passage of Scripture and told him the good news about Jesus.

As they traveled along the road, they came to some water and the eunuch said, "Look, here is water. Why shouldn't I be baptized?" And he gave orders to stop the chariot. Then both Philip and the eunuch went down into the water and Philip baptized him. (Acts 8:26-38)

It's easy to see why Philip is such a great example of a Talker. He walked by the carriage and created a natural conversation based on what the Ethiopian eunuch was interested in. He asked nonthreatening questions, started the discussion where the eunuch was at, and then explained the gospel story in a very natural and compelling way. The story was so gripping that when the Ethiopian finally got it, he wanted to pull over right away and get baptized as a Christian!

Talkers know how to "walk along beside the carriage" of their friends, listen for opportunities to bring up the gospel, and bring it up in a persuasive way. If you, like Philip, are a Talker, start looking for those everyday opportunities to bring up the gospel with your friends.

② STALKERS

Many of the most successful people in the universe were stalkers. And, no, I'm not talking about that evil kind of stalking where someone follows another person. I'm talking about those who stalk a singular goal relentlessly. You have stalker friends who win in sports, studies, and life because they are focused, bold, confident, and determined.

There are Stalkers in the faith-sharing world as well. They tend to be direct, blunt, and strong as they share the gospel. They are thought-provoking by their sheer boldness. What is their primary weakness? Sometimes they can turn people off with their bluntness and boldness.

The apostle Peter was a Stalker of sorts. Bold and direct, he unapologetically laid out the truth of the gospel in plain view for all to see. He was unstoppable in sharing Jesus.

Peter could be blunt in his sharing style (see Acts 2:14, 38). But he challenged people to consider Christ. Peter had a way of bringing people to a decision, either way, on the spot.

If you are a Stalker, you need to balance your sharing with love but realize that God has called you to be one of those catalytic proclaimers of truth who bring people to a decision through their unrelenting boldness.

③ BUDDIES

Buddies are those, like my wife, who are intensely and immensely relational. Sometimes Buddies confuse themselves with Talkers. But they are totally different. While Talkers love to . . . well, talk, Buddies love to listen. In the baseball world they would be more fielders than pitchers. They react to conversations instead of creating them.

When it comes to sharing the gospel, Buddies let the conversation unfold and gently guide it to Jesus. They ask a lot of questions and share a lot fewer answers. They share the message of Christ by tiny degrees in the midst of a conversation (or several) instead of bold declarations.

While there are several examples of Buddies in the Bible, there is one example, a guy named Barnabas (whose name actually means "son of encouragement"), who was really good at being a buddy. Check this passage out:

> When he [Saul] came to Jerusalem, he tried to join the disciples, but they were all afraid of him, not believing that he really was a disciple. But Barnabas took him and brought him to the apostles. He told them how Saul on his journey had seen the Lord and that the Lord had spoken to him, and how in Damascus he had preached fearlessly in the name of Jesus. (Acts 9:26-27)

So here's the deal. Before the great apostle Paul was the apostle Paul, he was a religious leader named Saul. He hated, persecuted, and chased Christians all over the place. But when Jesus showed up and knocked him off his donkey, so to speak, Saul became a Christian. Not only was his soul changed, but so was his name. Saul became Paul.

WARNING!

These styles of sharing the gospel are not hard and fast. You may find yourself as a combination of a few of them. The goal is to minimize your weaknesses, maximize your strengths, and use your style to advance the good news of Jesus while finding balance in your own style of evangelism.

So the newly converted Paul came to Jerusalem, the center of Christianity at that time, and tried to hang out with the other believers. Nobody wanted to. Most of them knew Paul when he was Saul, a persecutor of the church. Many of them probably thought that his conversion to Christianity was some kind of ploy to get on the inside of the church and really wreak havoc.

Nobody else but Barnabas listened to him. Barnabas took time to hear Paul's story and believed him. As a matter of fact, Barnabas is the one who took Paul and brought him personally to appear before the apostles to share his story with them.

Almost every time you see Barnabas in the book of Acts, he is fighting for the underdog. He is the one who listens to, loves, and empathizes with those around him.

While we don't ever see his sharing style per se, we can see clearly that he had a Buddy-bent. You can be sure that he was relational, loved to listen and serve, and shared the gospel in compassionate ways.

My wife is a Buddy. Her strength is that she loves and listens. Her weakness is that sometimes she is afraid to bring up the gospel with others.

If you are a Buddy you are blessed with a huge capacity for loving and listening. People love to talk to you because you love to listen—to *genuinely listen*—to them. You must resist the temptation to just listen. If you are going to become effective for Christ in sharing your faith, you must learn how to gently turn those conversations toward Jesus, as a fielder, not a pitcher; as a Barnabas, not a Paul.

4 BRAINS

Brains tend to be smart, organized, and intellectually stimulating (that leaves me out!). They are usually good at discussing and debating the claims of Christianity.

Luke was a Brain. He wrote two of the books of the Bible: Luke (duh!) and Acts. What is more, he wrote them to one guy, a Roman official named Theophilus. It seems as though Luke is making a case for Christianity in his first book and is demonstrating that it exploded across the world in his second one (Acts). Look how Luke describes his own style when it comes to communicating truth:

Many have undertaken to draw up an account of the things that have been fulfilled among us, just as they were handed down to us by those who from the first were eyewitnesses and servants of the word. Therefore, since I myself have carefully investigated everything from the beginning, it seemed good also to me to write an orderly account for you, most excellent Theophilus, so that you may know the certainty of the things you have been taught. (Luke 1:1-4)

Notice the phrases "carefully investigated everything" and "write an orderly account" and "that you may know the certainty of the things." In these phrases you see Luke's style. He studied. He was organized in his thoughts and words. And his goal was to prove to Theophilus that the things he was learning about Jesus were true!

Those who are Brains tend to do well laying out well-reasoned arguments for Christianity. They present the gospel message in an intellectually stimulating and logical way. Their weakness? They can tend to come off as cold and uncaring.

Just because you get good grades doesn't mean you are a Brain in this sense. Being a Brain is more of a personality type than it is an IQ test.

DISCOVERING YOUR STYLE

So how do you discover your personal sharing style?

First of all pray and ask God to give you wisdom to discern it. Remember the promise of James 1:5, "If any of you lacks wisdom, he should ask God, who gives generously to all without finding fault, and it will be given to him."

Secondly, your initial "gut instinct" is probably right. When you read the descriptions of the Talker, Stalker, Buddy, and Brain, which one did you initially think best matched you? Your first impression when it comes to things like this is usually right!

Finally, I developed a little nonscientific "test" to help you identify your personal style of sharing Jesus. Circle the answer that applies most to you:

1. Which word describes you the most?

   A. Funny

   B. Bold

   C. Caring

   D. Logical

2. "Sometimes I tend to . . .

   A. joke around too much."

   B. hurt people's feelings with my directness."

   C. worry about what other people think of me."

   D. get frustrated with others who don't 'get it' when it comes to thought problems and mental challenges."

3. Your friends would probably describe you as

   A. The life of the party

   B. The leader of the pack

C. A friend who really listens

D. The smart kid

4. If you had a friend you wanted to lead to Christ, which of the following things would you be more likely to do?

   A. Find the most creative way (using humor if possible) you could possibly use to bring up the gospel message.

   B. Just bring it up to him or her with a direct question.

   C. Take your friend to the video arcade and pray that it naturally comes up in the conversation.

   D. Give your friend a book or send him or her to a website that makes a strong, logical case for Christianity, and then talk about it afterward.

5. What makes you the most uncomfortable in a situation where you have the opportunity to share your faith?

   A. Not being able to bring it up in a natural and witty way

   B. Beating around the bush

   C. Making the other person feel uncomfortable

   D. Not having the answers if they ask hard questions

6. How would you bring up the gospel with total strangers?

   A. Get them laughing, get them talking, and then switch gears to Jesus naturally.

   B. Ask them if they know for sure they are going to heaven when they die.

   C. Try to talk to them and wait to see if they want to talk at all.

   D. Ask them questions about who they think Jesus was and if they are open to proof that He was the Son of God.

7. Which phrase below bests describes your style of sharing?

   A. Hey, bro! Listen to this!

B. Are you talking to me? Good, 'cause I wanna talk to you!

C. God gave us two ears and one mouth for a reason . . . to listen first!

D. Resistance to my brain power is futile!

8. "I tend to get in trouble for . . .

   A. too much joking."

   B. being too blunt."

   C. not much."

   D. arguing."

9. "If I were trying to motivate other Christians to share their faith, I would try to . . .

   A. talk them into it."

   B. take them out and do it with them."

   C. encourage them to build strong relationships with the lost first."

   D. teach them apologetics" (the art of "proving" Christianity through historical, scientific, or archeological facts, fulfilled prophecy, etc.).

Add up your score here:

Number of A's ____, B's____, C's____, D's _____.

If you are mostly A's then you may be a Talker—funny, creative, and "the life of the party" when it comes to sharing Jesus.

If you are mostly B's then you may be a "Stalker"—direct, bold, and "the leader of the pack" when it comes to sharing your faith.

CAN I GET A WITNESS?

I'm Rachael, 17, from Aurora, Colorado. I'm mostly a "Brain." I find ways to relate God to things I learn at school, like when we read Dante's Inferno or when we studied the Reformation. It's kind of like Paul did with the people in Athens who had an altar "to an unknown God." Other people are more like Peter, getting in front of a crowd and giving them the message bluntly. God blesses both approaches.

Scored mostly C's? Then you may be a Buddy—relational, kind, and a true friend when it comes to telling others about Jesus.

And if you marked mostly D's then you may be a Brain—smart, logical, and a person who can make a strong case for Christianity with your sheer logic.

WHICH STYLE DID JESUS USE?

Jesus shows us the ultimate balance of all four sharing styles! We see Him being a Talker throughout the synoptic gospels (Matthew, Mark, and Luke) as He uses short, fictional stories called "parables" to share His message in creative, thought-provoking, and, sometimes, funny ways. We see Him being a "Stalker" in Matthew 23 when He takes on the religious leaders boldly in the temple and challenges their belief system and behavior without flinching. We see Jesus being a "Buddy" in John 4 when He broke cultural taboos to talk to a Samaritan woman, treat her with dignity and respect, and share with her the "living water" (aka "the gospel"). Finally we see Jesus as a "Brain" in Luke 24 when, after His resurrection, He used passages in the Old Testament to prove that He had to die and rise again from the dead.

Everybody has a unique sharing style!

TALKER

Description: Creative, funny, inspiring

Strengths: Articulate, persuasive

Weakness: Might be afraid to offend

Biblical Example: Phillip

STALKER

Description: Direct, blunt, strong, thought-provoking

Strengths: Bold, courageous, consistent

Weakness: Can turn people off

Biblical Example: Peter

BUDDY

Description: Relational, compassionate servant

Strengths: Loves and listens

Weakness: May be afraid to bring it up

Biblical Example: Barnabas

BRAIN

Description: Smart and organized, intellectual

Strengths: Logical

Weakness: Can be non-emotional and cold

Biblical Example: Luke

As you can see from this graph, the four sharing styles are centered on Jesus! He is the ultimate balance that you should be seeking to achieve when it comes to sharing His message. What does this mean for you as you recognize your sharing style?

Three things:

1. Keep your eyes on Jesus!

As you grow and mature in Christ you will find yourself "spilling over" into other styles. When I first started sharing my faith as a Talker/Stalker mix I thought that my style was the best. But as I've kept my eyes on Jesus over the years, I've become more balanced, hopefully more like Jesus, as I've shared my faith.

2. Maximize your strengths and minimize your weaknesses!

Every style has built-in strengths and weaknesses. Whether you are bold, funny, relational, or logical, use it! Just realize your built-in weaknesses and minimize them as much as possible!

3. Learn to use different styles in different situations!

If you are a Buddy and you are standing at a bus stop with a complete stranger, you don't have time to build a friendship. Venture out and do what a Talker would do: Try to bring up the gospel in a funny or creative way! If you are a Stalker and you just became part of the basketball team, try not giving the gospel in the first team huddle. You have all season long. Try being a Buddy/Stalker mix. Aggressively pursue one-on-one opportunities to build relationships and then bring it up!

A FINAL THOUGHT

Although the Bible doesn't flatly state that there are different styles of sharing the gospel, these styles are clearly seen throughout the New Testament. No one style is better than another. As a matter of fact, ultimately, the sharing style you have is not the most important issue. The most important thing is that you are lovingly communicating the gospel message in the power of the Spirit for the glory of God.

But now the question is, how do you get started sharing the gospel with your friends? How do you bring it up without throwing up?

PART TWO:
SHARING YOUR FAITH

chapter 7

HOW TO BRING IT UP
WITHOUT THROWING UP

You are sitting across from your friend in the school cafeteria.
Nobody else is at your table. The conversation "tone" is perfect.
You are both talking in that strange friend zone where you
know that you can bring up any subject and talk about it. You're
committed to living THE Cause out loud in your life and you've
been waiting and praying for the opportunity to tell your friend
about Jesus. And here it is. So what do you do? How do you bring
it up without throwing up?

There is no easy answer to this question. Why? Not because
there's no simple way to initiate a conversation about God, but
because there are a thousand ways to get the conversation started!

MOVING INTO A SPIRITUAL CONVERSATION

Smoothly and naturally moving a conversation from a casual,
everyday subject to topics like God, sin, and salvation is an art
to be learned. And we learn it by watching how the best of the
best did it in the pages of Scripture. Who is the best? Of course,

Jesus! Check out where He graciously and skillfully shifts the conversation from a cup of water to the spiritual realm in John 4:6-14:

> Jesus, tired as he was from the journey, sat down by [Jacob's] well. It was about the sixth hour.
>
> When a Samaritan woman came to draw water, Jesus said to her, "Will you give me a drink?" (His disciples had gone into the town to buy food.)
>
> The Samaritan woman said to him, "You are a Jew and I am a Samaritan woman. How can you ask me for a drink?" (For Jews do not associate with Samaritans.)
>
> Jesus answered her, "If you knew the gift of God and who it is that asks you for a drink, you would have asked him and he would have given you living water."
>
> "Sir," the woman said, "you have nothing to draw with and the well is deep. Where can you get this living water? Are you greater than our father Jacob, who gave us the well and drank from it himself, as did also his sons and his flocks and herds?"
>
> Jesus answered, "Everyone who drinks this water will be thirsty again, but whoever drinks the water I give him will never thirst. Indeed, the water I give him will become in him a spring of water welling up to eternal life."

Jesus was breaking cultural taboos even talking with this Samaritan woman, but He did it anyway. He loved her and wanted her to know the joy of the forgiveness that He had to offer.

When she was talking about water in the liquid form, Jesus was talking about spiritual water. Just as a cold drink of water can satisfy your thirst on a hot day, Jesus can satisfy your soul in a world of pain and disappointment. The difference is that with Jesus, once you drink of Him, you will never thirst again for anything else—He's the ultimate thirst quencher.

Keep your eyes on Jesus, stay filled with His Spirit and alert to the everyday opportunities that God has granted, and you too can learn to move the conversation from an everyday subject toward something spiritual.

> **WARNING!**
>
> Be careful when moving conversations from the ordinary to the extraordinary. Try to make your efforts to shift the conversation toward God as smooth as possible, not forced. For instance, if somebody says to you, "It's sure hot in here," don't say, "It's hot in hell, too!" Be as sensitive and smooth as possible when you make a transition from your everyday conversation to eternal matters.

Here are a few hints to help you learn how to move your conversations toward God more and more:

PRAY FOR OPEN EYES TO SEE THE OPPORTUNITIES EVERY DAY

Right after Jesus shared the "living water" with the woman at the well, the disciples came and wondered what was going on. Jesus told them to open their spiritual eyes to see the people all around them who desperately needed to hear and believe the gospel. Using another analogy, Jesus rebukes them in John 4:35 by commanding them, "Open your eyes and look at the fields! They are ripe for harvest."

CAN I GET A WITNESS?

My name is Melody. I am 14 and I live in Kansas City, Kansas. I've been talking to one of my friends about church and stuff and trying to tell her about Christ through two bands' music…She is going through struggles with her parents and cutting, and she really wants someone to talk to. I've been praying for her and brought her to church once and have been trying to use music to talk about my faith.

Jesus wants you to be aware of those who are spiritually ripe and ready all around you every single day. Pray for open eyes to see the opportunities that are already there at school, work, home, and play.

LOOK FOR "THE FORK IN THE ROAD"

While you are in conversation, look for what I call "the fork in the road." What is that? It's the point in the conversation where you can turn it one direction or the other. You can turn down the highway of everyday banter about life, sports, movies, music, friends, blah, blah, blah. Or you can take the turn at the fork in the road toward more spiritual subjects.

For instance, let's say you are talking to a friend about a teacher. Maybe this is your favorite teacher. She always has a great attitude and is willing to serve. Then you suddenly remember that she is a Christian. You can take the highway of everyday blah, blah, blah, or you can take the turn toward the more awkward by saying something like, "Maybe one of the reasons she has such a good attitude is because she is in tune with God on a deeper level." From there you can continue down the road of spiritual discussion to the point where you are listening to your friend's spiritual beliefs and sharing yours.

Here is a list of conversational topics and examples of how you can take the turn at the fork in the road to move toward God-talk:

Them:	You:
"I love that song!"	"Yeah, it's sweet! Does that one line ever get you wondering about God when you hear it?"
"I really liked that movie. It was awesome!"	"Me too! The characters seemed real. They hurt and struggled just like in real life. Do you ever wonder why there's so much crap in the world?"
"I just lost my aunt to cancer."	"I'm sorry. Does it make you wonder about what it takes to get into heaven when you die?"
"I can't believe she back-stabbed me like that."	"I know it hurts when somebody treats you bad. Do you ever take your hurt feelings to God and ask Him how you should respond?"
"How much do you bench-press?"	"Two-fifty. But to me there is a whole lot of stuff more important than how much you bench."
"That news story was really disturbing."	"I agree. Where do you turn when you're afraid or freaked out by something?"
"I hate my dad! He's only into himself."	"I'm so sorry. I guess that's why I'm so thankful for my heavenly dad."

On and on the list goes. As a matter of fact, I'm convinced that any conversation, anytime, can eventually be shifted to the subject of salvation. Just be aware and watch for the fork in the road.

GO FOR IT IN LOVE!

Okay, let's say that you are in the midst of a conversation waiting for that natural fork in the road to appear. It doesn't. What do you do? Of course you must be sensitive to the Holy Spirit's leading, but since God has laid it on your heart to share your faith with this person, I would encourage you to go for it anyway. How? Simply say something like, "Would you mind if I changed the subject?"

Subjects change all the time in the natural ebb and flow of teen conversations anyway. Once you change the subject, just bring it up. There are several kinds of opening questions you can

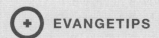 **EVANGETIPS**

If you are in a small group of Christian teenagers, you can all "practice" making conversational transitions to God-talk by doing a little game that I used to play when I was a teenager. Somebody would pick a subject, any subject, and the first person to make the most natural transition toward the subject of salvation wins. Subjects like a ketchup bottle, a football game, a diamond ring, or a big, steaming pile of manure can be used as subjects. Believe it or not, this little, goofy game will sharpen your abilities to move toward spiritual conversations every day!

use to launch into a spiritual conversation and they generally work well because they tap into people's natural desire to talk about themselves and their opinions. Identifying the questions you're most comfortable using generally depends on your own unique sharing style.

OPENING QUESTIONS

If you are a Talker (creative, funny, persuasive) then some opening questions you may feel more comfortable using include the following:

- "Do you believe in God?"
- "What do you think God wants from you?"
- "Would it surprise you to know that God wants a relationship with you that starts now and lasts forever?"

If you're a Stalker (direct, bold, relentless) then some opening questions you may feel more comfortable using could be:

- "Where are you at when it comes to God and religion?"
- "Can I tell you why I believe it's more about a relationship with God and not about a religion?"

If you're a Buddy (relational, loving, kind) then your opening questions could be:

- "Would you tell me about your spiritual journey so far?"
- "Would you mind telling me about yourself and what is important to you?"
- "Can you share with me your view of God?"

If you're a Brain (logical, smart, convincing) then you could ask:

- "Who do you think Jesus was—God Himself, a good teacher, or something else?"
- "What do you believe about God and why?"
- "Why do you think there are so many different religions? Do you think they can all be right?"

These are just samples and examples of opening questions you could use, depending on your primary style of sharing your faith. There is no perfect list because there are no perfect questions. But sometimes you've just got to bring it up. When you do, remember this verse in 1 Peter 4:8: "Above all, love each other deeply, because love covers over a multitude of sins." As long as you make whatever transition toward the gospel in love—awkward, smooth, or otherwise—people will usually cut you slack.

So identify some questions that you feel comfortable using, pray for open eyes to see the opportunities all around you every day, look for the most natural "fork in the road," and when all else fails just bring it up in love. If you feel fear rising, let it remind you to pray, because when you pray, you get back in the "power zone" of being controlled by God's Spirit. It's only when we are Spirit-empowered that we can be fully used by God to advance the kingdom of God in power! Then move into it, even if the idea of sharing Jesus with somebody makes your palms

CAN I GET A WITNESS?

I'm Jim. I'm 15, from Lawrenceville, Georgia. Here's the thing man, no matter how much we are scared, God is always with us. Why should we be scared someone is going to make fun of us when we know that the Lord our God is there always? Who cares what other people say about you? What matters is that you know that God is always with you, no matter what, and that you took a stand for your beliefs.

sweat and your heart race. Don't hold back. Just push the words out of your mouth to trigger the conversation. After that it will be a whole lot easier to talk about heaven, hell, life, purpose, Jesus, sin, and hope.

But after you bring it up and get the conversation launched, you need to know what to say next. You need to be equipped to take your friends through the whole story of the gospel.

chapter 8

HOW TO SHARE THE
WHOLE STORY OF THE GOSPEL

Have you ever been on a backpacking trip in the mountains? Being from Colorado, I've had the privilege of traversing the beautiful, rugged, and sometimes dangerous Rocky Mountains from time to time.

Experienced backpackers and rock climbers know that you enter these mountains with a mixture of fear and excitement. Take them too lightly and you could end up neck deep in an avalanche or as a puddle of gush at the bottom of a cliff.

In a lot of ways sharing the gospel with somebody is like taking them on a journey to the crest of a distant mountain. At the top of the mountain awaits a restored relationship with the God of the universe that starts now and lasts forever. The problem is that between you and your final destination lie many dangers, the biggest of which is a huge, seemingly unbridgeable chasm. If you can get your friend across this Grand Canyon–sized hole in the earth, then their powerful and permanent relationship with God is secure and their faith in Jesus will provide the assurance of salvation and the hope of heaven. If you can't, then he or she will never experience the view from the top of the mountain on the other side of the chasm.

God has equipped you with a backpack filled with everything you need to take your friend on this exciting and exhausting journey. Your compass is the Holy Spirit. Your map is the Word of God. And you are the guide.

Your goal is to help your friend find a way across this gigantic chasm to God. The challenge is that there is only one way across. Jesus claimed to be "the way and the truth and the life." He is the only way across and you must help your friend find Him.

The challenge is this: How do you convince your friend to take the journey in the first place? This becomes especially tricky when you consider that your friend may already be way off course or on a different pathway altogether. If your friend is steeped in Mormonism or Islam, for example, there is a good chance that he or she is way down the wrong road, headed toward the wrong destination.

You may have some friends who are well on their way down the path toward eternal life but have stalled out for some reason. For instance, if your friend was raised in a solid church that preached the gospel, yet for some reason or another has never trusted in Christ, he or she may be stalled out somewhere along their way to trusting in Jesus. Perhaps all your friend needs is a little encouragement from you to continue the journey.

All of your friends, classmates, and teammates, even the atheist ones, are on a spiritual journey toward somewhere. The question is, how do we get them on the one path that leads to a restored relationship with God and eternal life? How do we get them across the chasm and on their way toward heaven?

A JOURNEY I'LL NEVER FORGET

A few years back, I took the journey of a lifetime with a group of teenagers whom I had never met before. There was Andy the atheist jock who loved to discuss why he didn't believe in the existence of a God. There was Ashley, the ex-Jehovah's Witness, who had many questions about the whole gospel message. There was Tasondra the city girl, Eric the Episcopalian, Ben the Presbyterian, and Tiffany the minister's daughter. One of the more colorful characters was Stephén. He was a Cajun Wiccan teenager who carried a chip on his shoulder and had a smart-aleck comment for everyone about everything.

The *GOSPEL Journey Adventure* cast group shot after a full day hiking in the Rockies (left to right: Tasondra, Eric, Zane, Stéphen, Tiffany, Ashley, Ben and Andy.)

these seven very diverse kids on a six-day adventure in
ado mountains for a kind of reality TV-type experience.
Whil___ ___y friend Zane guided them through the mountain
adventures (rock climbing, white-water rafting, rappelling),
I guided them through the story of the gospel as it unfolded
throughout the Bible.

We used a simple acrostic as our road map through the
biblical truths. Sometimes students get intimidated by the Bible
and the long sweep of history that it covers. But the "big" story
of the Bible can be explained in a few key truths that capture
the essence of God and human interaction. The simple six letter
acrostic we used explains the gospel in way those unfamiliar
with the Bible can understand.

The acrostic spells out the word "GOSPEL" and communicates
the key truths of the gospel message as they span the whole story
of the Bible. It goes like this:

The GOSPEL Journey® Message

G od created us to be with Him.

O ur sins separate us from God.

S ins cannot be removed by good deeds.

P aying the price for sin, Jesus died and rose again.

E veryone who trusts in Him alone has eternal life.

L ife with Jesus starts now and lasts forever.

Every day our group did some kind of new and exciting challenge, and we tied that day's adventure into one of the sessions for the day. For instance, after a get-to-know-you hike high above the Continental Divide, I talked about **G**—the fact that **G**od created us to be with Him. In this session I shared what the Word of God said about who we are and how we got here. I painted a picture of God's original intent for humankind before Satan slithered in and it all came crashing down. In this first session I talked about the doctrine of the Trinity, creation versus evolution, the image of God in people, and more. I then opened it up for questions, arguments, and discussions . . . which triggered great spiritual conversations!

The next five points covered the rest of the gospel story as it unfolded throughout the rest of the Bible. We talked through the Ten Commandments, the sacrificial system outlined in the Old Testament, the birth of Christ, and much more. These teenagers never once seemed to get bored. Although we were covering full-out theology, they realized that our spiritual conversations had major implications for some of the core issues of life: relationships, purpose, sin, forgiveness, redemption, and hope. All the teenagers were fully engaged. It didn't hurt that we were able to use powerful visual illustrations like the Continental Divide, a sheer rock wall, or a ropes course to make our points.

What happened over the course of six days amazed me. The intense discussions spilled over into the SUV rides, the rafting trip, and the hot tub!

Three of the kids who came with us were already Christians when they began the journey. I had the privilege of helping two of the remaining four students across the chasm into a personal relationship with Jesus Christ. Being a part of their journey to

Jesus was one of the most spiritually rewarding experiences I have ever had!

And you can take your friends on the GOSPEL Journey too. As you understand and master the six parts of this message, you'll be prepared to unfold this powerful message to them in a relevant and loving way.

In the next six, short chapters, let me be your guide through the GOSPEL Journey Message. Let's continue the backpacking analogy as we take a look, one-by-one, at the key truths summarized in the GOSPEL.

This unscripted Rocky Mountain adventure was captured on film and developed into a reality series. Available through Dare 2 Share Ministries, *GOSPEL Journey Adventure* is designed to be used as a small group curriculum. The students' unforgettable quest to understand the gospel message straight from the pages of Scripture unfolds with raw, real, and riveting discussions.

A second *GOSPEL Journey* reality series was filmed in Maui. Using a Craigslist ad, Dare 2 Share pulled together seven young strangers representing seven very different worldviews. *GOSPEL Journey Maui* captured their intense and intentional spiritual conversation when they were thrown together in a Maui beach house for a week.

For more information regarding these two *GOSPEL Journey* reality series, visit dare2share.org/store or see page 284.

chapter 9

GOD CREATED US TO BE WITH HIM

Our trip starts out on a beautiful day. The trek we take up the steep mountain path is laced with flowers and takes us through dense forests. Lush plants and trees line both sides of the narrow walkway. The sound of chirping birds, buzzing bees, and ribbiting frogs fill the forest around us. This teeming jungle in the mountains is alive with life in all shapes and sizes. So far so good.

✛ ✛ ✛

THE FIRST GARDEN

In some ways that's probably what Adam and Eve experienced in the Garden of Eden so many years ago. They were surrounded by sheer beauty, which was unscathed by the ravages of sin. They too were on a journey, not an earthy path through the jungle, but a spiritual quest to please God in this brand-new adventure called "life." And speaking of life, it was teeming all around and above them.

TASONDRA'S EYES OPEN

I wish you could have seen Tasondra's eyes when she saw the beauty of the Continental Divide in the Rocky Mountains from the top of a huge mountain. I think it was her first time above timberline (so high that trees don't grow there). This city girl understood all about magnificent buildings and the complexities of living in the city. But to experience the rush and thrill of the majestic views toward the top of a Colorado peak left her speechless and breathless (the air is much thinner 13,000 feet up!).

It was as if she were the first person to ever behold God's creation—a new Eve, if you will, dumbstruck by the beauty of the garden. The moment was broken, however, when a group of mountain bikers pedaled up and stopped to catch their breath. She was suddenly snapped back to her quick-witted, funny, city-girl self. But still, Tasondra's heart had sensed the call of creation, and it struck a chord in her soul. That momentary peace she had felt was meant to last forever. God's original intention had been so good.

God had created pristine lakes, vast oceans, never-ending forests, and the shockingly beautiful Garden of Eden as the setting for Adam and Eve to enjoy. The sun shone its warm rays on their naked skin at just the right temperature. It never got too hot in the daytime. It never got too cold at night. The food was great. The animals were tame. Everything was, well, perfect.

Adam and Eve were open, honest, innocent, and as naked as jaybirds. (*How did that expression start anyway? Come on, isn't a jaybird as naked as other birds out there? Don't feathers count as clothes? But I digress.*)

These two sin-free beings experienced everything God originally intended for all mankind to experience. They had no fights, no disagreements, only love, peace, and absolute harmony. They found significance in the tending of the garden. They found security in a strong relationship with God and with each other. It was truly paradise on earth.

GOOD NEWS, BAD NEWS

The good news is that God's original plan was that all humanity would be happy, healthy, and holy, in perfect relationship with their Creator. The bad news (which we'll soon see in the next chapter) is that the whole deal got messed up by sin. As a result there are death, sin, war, crime, broken relationships, busted dreams, and pain in the world.

Most people don't know that God created them so that He could pour His love out on them. Adam and Eve had everything our world is looking and longing for so badly. Physically, emotionally, spiritually, and socially they were completely fulfilled.

Stop and think of what your friends are looking for in life. Adam and Eve had it all.

> *"Know that the Lord is God. It is he who made us, and we are his."*
>
> **(Psalm 100:3a)**

Many people today are on a quest for physical fitness. Adam was so healthy that even after he was condemned to die, he still lived hundreds of years (Genesis 5:4).

People want a job that's fulfilling. Adam and Eve had that. God gave them three jobs

Nothing like an early morning hike and great conversation!

to do. They were to take care of the Garden of Eden (Genesis 2:15), rule over the animal kingdom, and fill the earth with their children and their children's children (Genesis 1:28).

They want emotional fulfillment. Adam and Eve had pure, unblushing emotional fulfillment. Nude wasn't crude in the Garden of Eden. It was a sign of transparency, honesty, and purity.

They want sex. Adam and Eve had it. It was God sanctioned unbridled, unhindered passion.

They want wealth and power. Adam and Eve had power over the entire world and everything in it. Has anyone else in history even come close to that?

Spiritually Adam and Eve walked with God, they talked with God, and they were with God. He was not hiding behind a veil in a temple or a cloud on a mountain or a burning bush to shield His glory from frail humanity. He was with them. They didn't shrink in terror from His glorious presence because they had no reason to run. They literally hung out with God, like you do with your friends after school.

Aren't all these things what the typical person today is looking for? Physical health; wealth and power; emotional, vocational, relational, and spiritual fulfillment. Yes, Adam and Eve had it all.

Then sin came walking in and everything got twisted.

On this first stage of our journey up the mountain, the sky overhead is an intense, breathtaking, brilliant blue. Sunlight filters through the trees, giving the lush forest around us a fresh, sparkling appearance. The patches of shade are cool and refreshing. We feel safe, secure, and satisfied. But off in the distance beyond our field of vision, dark clouds are gathering that will wreak havoc on our perfect surroundings. A storm is brewing that will soon soak the terrain with pain, shame, and sin.

chapter 10

Our sins
SEPARATE US FROM GOD

As we continue on the beautiful path filled with the luscious plants of God's love, weeds start to sprout before our eyes. For the first time we see a dead carcass of some animal by the pathway. It reeks of death—new death—death that was earned by the sin of Adam and Eve.

A storm begins to gather as we approach a huge cliff. The chasm wasn't there before, and the horizon looks strange and eerie now. We tremble when we realize the cliff cuts off our path to eternal life. Across the deep, dark, fog-filled valley beneath us we can barely see the continuation of the path on the other side. It looks like it's a mile or so away. There's no way we can get from here to there.

The whole thing looks like a huge chunk of earth has dropped off into the abyss. What's left is an uncrossable chasm that the strongest arm in football couldn't throw across on his best day.

✦ ✦ ✦

THE CONSEQUENCES OF THE FIRST SIN

The chasm was created when Adam and Eve sinned. On one side of the chasm are sin, death, and hopelessness. On the other side is eternal life. This huge, gaping, Grand Canyon–sized hole represents the separation that began when Adam and Eve sinned for the first time.

Adam and Eve knew and enjoyed the presence and purity of God in the Garden of Eden. When they chose to sin (by eating the forbidden fruit), a chasm was created. This hole can't be filled. It's much too big. It can't be crossed. It's far too wide. It represents the immeasurable distance between a holy, sinless God and a selfish, sinful humanity.

When Adam and Eve ate of the forbidden fruit, something deadly took place inside the inner caverns of their souls. They were corrupted. They became depraved. The cancer of selfishness and disease of pride spread throughout every fiber of their spiritual beings. Once destined to rule the earth, they now became slaves to sin and Satan.

What was their first reaction after disobeying God?

To cover their shame!

Genesis 3:7 explains the sad aftermath of their sinful choices: "Then the eyes of both of them were opened, and they realized they were naked; so they sewed fig leaves together and made coverings for themselves."

Their second reaction?

To hide from God!

Genesis 3:8-9 puts it this way: "Then the man and his wife heard the sound of the Lord God as he was walking in the garden

Greg spends some time at every stop reflecting on
what the Bible says about the issue for that day.

in the cool of the day, and they hid from the Lord God among the
trees of the garden. But the Lord God called to the man, 'Where
are you?'"

The rest of the Bible describes a cosmic hide-and-go-seek
game where God searches for us, for humanity, but we are still
hiding in the gardens of religion, philosophy, materialism, or
hedonism. Yet God has never stopped calling out "Where are
you?" to a lost, depraved, and hiding world.

Adam and Eve's third reaction?

To play the blame game!

Man blames the woman. Woman blames the serpent. By this
time the whole of paradise had unraveled irreparably. Sin was at
the root of all of this tragedy. What was the end result of this one
sinful choice? Broken relationships, busted dreams, shattered
lives, and death.

Believe it or not, Adam's sin is the reason corruption, famine, crime, and war steal the newspaper headlines. Scripture tells us in Romans 5:12, "Therefore, just as sin entered the world through one man, and death through sin, and in this way death came to all men, because all sinned—"

Adam was mankind's spiritual representative before God. When he sinned, he sinned on our behalf. If the President declares war on some country then we, as Americans, declare war as well. The President is our political representative and acts on our behalf whether we like it or not.

STEPHÉN, MY WILD, WICCAN FRIEND

Of all the participants of the *GOSPEL Journey,* Stephén was the wildest, proudest, and loudest. He attacked every day with a smile and a determination to win whatever competition we would have that day.

During the teaching times he would ask a lot of questions and make a lot of comments, almost to the point of dominating the Q&A time. At first many of the other participants were irritated by him. But Stephén grew on everybody. He was a nice kid with a small frame, a big mouth—and a big heart to match!

During one of the teaching times, I had everybody take a mirror and look into it for 10 seconds. I asked everyone to think of one thing they had done in the last 12 months that they were ashamed of, that God was ashamed of. When I asked at the end of this experience how it had made them feel, Stephén was completely honest and vulnerable. He shared how guilty he felt, how much he sensed that he was an absolute sinner in that moment. Now, you have to understand, this was significant—Wiccans don't really believe in sin. But in that moment Stephén did. My loud, proud, little friend got quiet, and I think he heard the footsteps of God coming in the distance.

The same is true of Adam. When he declared war on God through his singular act of rebellion, he was acting as our spiritual representative. As a result, whether we like it or not, all of us declared war on God as well.

Through Adam's defiance of God's one simple command, the floodgates of sin were opened. As a result, from the womb to the tomb we are soaked in sin. It drenches our thoughts and motives. It seeps through our words and actions. It drowns our lives and relationships.

This sin nature can also be compared to cancer. It corrupted the very DNA of our souls. Adam's sin spread like a genetic defect to every one of his children and their children's children until it made its way to you and me.

When explaining the gospel to someone, it is important to explain the relationship that God created mankind to enjoy with Him and how sin ruined that beautiful unity. Since the day that Eve gave birth to Cain, mankind has been born kicking and screaming, selfish and sinful, mutinous and murderous. It's in our blood. We have all fallen from the dysfunctional family tree called depravity.

FIRE AND BRIMSTONE

The ultimate consequence of this separation from God is eternal separation from Him in a literal place called hell. Perhaps the saddest and scariest phrase in Scripture is lodged in 2 Thessalonians 1:7-9: "[Jesus will appear] in blazing fire with his powerful angels. He will punish those who do not know God and do not obey the gospel of our Lord Jesus. They will be punished with everlasting destruction and shut out from the presence of the Lord and from the majesty of his power."

Think about those words "shut out from the presence of the Lord." The scariest thing about hell is not the presence of darkness or flame or pain but the absence of hope and love and Jesus. If this doesn't break your heart for the lost, check your pulse, because you might be dead.

Hell is scary. It represents something even more intimidating than fire and flame. It stands for God's hatred for sin. Hell burns forever because God's hatred of wickedness burns forever. It takes an eternity of flame to quench God's holy disdain of that which is evil.

> *"For all have sinned and fall short of the glory of God."*
>
> **(Romans 3:23)**

It is vital that we help our friends who don't know Christ realize that the relationship God wanted to enjoy with all of us in Genesis 1 was completely ruined by sin in Genesis 3. When sin came walking in, communion with God went running out.

And there's nothing you can do about that.

So here we are, stuck on one side of the valley of the shadow of death created by Adam and Eve's sinful choice. A cold, harsh wind whips about us. We pull out our rain gear, and suddenly the storm clouds unleash their torrents. But our gear is inadequate to protect us from the fury of the storm and we are soon drenched and shivering. In our misery and despair we realize that if we are to continue the GOSPEL Journey, we have to find a way across the gaping chasm.

chapter 11

Sins cannot be
REMOVED BY GOOD DEEDS

*This fog-filled hole looming before us presents a big problem.
We start to strategize how we can get across and continue our
journey. We think,* "Well, I'm a pretty good distance jumper.
Maybe if I got a running start . . ." *then we look across the
gargantuan chasm and think again.*

"Maybe I can attach a rope to a spear of some kind and
drive it into a tree or something on the other side. It could be the
beginning of a bridge of some sort."

*But down deep inside we finally come to the grim realization
there is no way to cross it on our own. We can't make it.*

+   +   +

ON THE WRONG SIDE OF THE CHASM

This is the same realization every person must have when it
comes to gaining eternal life. More often than not, people think

they can cross the chasm of sin by being a good person. Take a survey among your classmates and you may be surprised. Just ask them one simple question: "What does it take to get to heaven?" You'll probably get answers that include the following:

> "I think I'm a pretty good person."
>
> "I try to live by the Ten Commandments."
>
> "I have been going to church all of my life."
>
> "I have never killed anybody or anything like that."

Most teenagers think that if they live a good life and are a nice person, then those behaviors in some way will get them across to heaven. They are steeped in a good-works mentality that says you can earn your way into heaven through acts of religious devotion or social justice, or even by being a halfway decent human being.

According to the Bible, there are at least two big problems with this line of thinking.

Big Problem No. 1:
One sin is enough to condemn you to hell.

James 2:10 puts it this way: "For whoever keeps the whole law and yet stumbles at just one point is guilty of breaking all of it." In other words, the Ten Commandments are a package deal. You bust one, you've fallen short of the package deal. You take on one, you take on all the others . . . and lose.

Romans 3:10-12 quotes the Old Testament and paints a bleak picture of how far short every single human falls:

> "There is no one righteous, not even one;
> there is no one who understands,

no one who seeks God.
All have turned away,
they have together become worthless;
there is no one who does good,
not even one."

The standard of getting into heaven is perfection—not just being good by the world's standards.

Big Problem No. 2:
Your good deeds can't make up for your bad ones.

First, God knows what we do and why we do it. Our good deeds may not be really so good. What look like good deeds on the outside can be springing forth from a heart filled with selfish, sinful motives.

Secondly, we can't work our way to heaven by doing more good than we do evil. Our holy and perfect God doesn't weigh our good deeds against our bad on a scale to see if we can squeak by with a 51%. God doesn't even grade on the curve, because perfection is His standard for a perfect and holy heaven.

From Genesis 4 all the way through Revelation, the Bible shows that our sins could never be removed by good deeds. Every person ever born (except Jesus) has sinned. Ephesians 5:5 makes it clear that "no immoral, impure or greedy person . . . has any inheritance in the kingdom of Christ and of God."

> *"All of us have become like one who is unclean, and all our righteous acts are like filthy rags."*
>
> **(Isaiah 64:6a)**

We all lie. We all lust. We all hate. We all covet. We all miss the mark on a daily basis. Only those who are as righteous as the Father Himself can be a part of the celestial kingdom. That means we are stuck on the wrong side of the chasm, and in and of ourselves, there's not a thing we can do about it.

THE TEN COMMANDMENTS

Sometimes people can't see their own sin until you hold up God's measuring stick. What is that? The Ten Commandments are one measure of God's standards. These were the 10 nonnegotiables that God required of the Israelites (and of us!).

Here they are as listed in Exodus 20:3-17:

1. You shall have no other gods before me.

    Have you ever put somebody else before God?

    +

2. You shall not make for yourself an idol in the form of anything in heaven above or on the earth beneath or in the waters below.

    Have you ever put something else before God?

    +

3. You shall not misuse the name of the Lord your God.

    Have you ever used the name of God in vain by saying "God _____!" or "Jesus Christ!" or "God!" in anger?

    +

4. Remember the Sabbath day by keeping it holy.

    Do you take one day a week to rest and reflect on God?

    +

5. Honor your father and mother.

Have you always honored the wishes of your parents with a good attitude? Uh oh!

+

6. You shall not murder.

Have you ever murdered somebody? Before you answer that, remember that the Bible says that if you hate somebody you've broken the spirit of this command (1 John 3:15). Oops!

+

7. You shall not commit adultery.

Have you sinned sexually with a member of the opposite or same sex? Remember that Jesus tells us in Matthew 5:28 that if we've lusted in our minds, we have broken this command in the eyes of God. Not good.

+

8. You shall not steal.

Have you ever stolen anything? What about time from your employer by surfing the Internet on company time? What about illegal downloading? What about stealing attention during class or stealing glory for somebody else's accomplishments?

+

9. You shall not give false testimony against your neighbor.

Have you ever lied about anything to anybody including exaggerations and "little white lies"?

+

10. You shall not covet your neighbor's house. You shall not covet your neighbor's wife, or his manservant or maidservant, his ox or donkey, or anything that belongs to your neighbor.

> *Have you ever coveted what somebody else had? Somebody's looks, strength, car, cash, girlfriend, or boyfriend?*

+

If we're honest, we'd admit that we break most of these commands a lot of the time. The problem is this: To get into heaven trying to obey the Ten Commandments, we would have

ANDY . . . MY NICE NEMESIS

Out of all the students who participated in the *GOSPEL Journey* project, Andy challenged me the most. Don't get me wrong, he was a very nice young man. I guess because he was so athletic, I wasn't ready for a mind that was every bit as chiseled as his body. Andy was always the first to question what I was communicating from the Bible. He asked any question that a well-educated atheist adult twice his age would ask. But he asked each question with tremendous respect.

One of the points Andy had the hardest time with was the Bible's contention that our sins cannot be removed by good deeds. If there was a heaven, he assumed it was for those who were good enough to enter, no matter what their religion. He talked to me several times about this problem that he just couldn't reconcile in his quick-witted mind.

Andy did well in all the high ropes and rappelling type challenges because of his athleticism. But the best challenge was the one he gave me every time I shared the gospel message.

to obey all of them perfectly all of the time from the moment we were born until the second that we died!

As you share your faith with your friends, you may find that some of them think they are already good enough to make it into heaven. If they do, try nudging them to consider they might be wrong about that assumption by using this Ten Commandments test on them, and they'll soon discover that they are not. But make sure you admit you are a sinner too. Once they realize they aren't "good enough," they may be more open to the idea that they need God's forgiveness that's available through Jesus.

And don't underestimate the power of prayer, for it is the Spirit of God's job to convict and convince. He convicts your friends of sin and convinces them that Jesus is who He claimed to be. Jesus reassures us in John 16:8 that when the Spirit of God comes, "he will convict the world of guilt in regard to sin and righteousness and judgment."

Your prayers unleash His power to convict and convince your friends. Pray, knowing that the Spirit of God can open hearts to make them receptive to the gospel!

Just as we realize that we can never make it across the chasm through our own efforts, the raging storm begins to abate. The heavy clouds begin to break apart and the dense fog filling the abyss that blocks our path begins to lift. We can now vaguely make out a rope bridge that spans the huge chasm. We can't help but notice that this little, narrow bridge is drenched blood-red . . . and we wonder why.

chapter 12

PAYING THE PRICE FOR SIN, JESUS DIED AND ROSE AGAIN

Intrigued, we make our way toward the mysterious rope bridge stretching across the massive chasm. Hope rises up inside us, but doubts creep into our minds as well. Is the bridge ahead an elusive mirage? If it is real, how did it get here? Why does it appear to be drenched in blood? Will it be sturdy enough to support us? The questions bombard us as we struggle to keep our footing on the wet, slippery pathway overlooking the chasm. We push back our fear and continue moving cautiously forward, seeking answers.

✜ ✜ ✜

THE GOD-MAN

Two thousand years ago in the small village of Bethlehem, God became the God-man. Fully God and fully man. Jesus was born the Son of God and the Son of Man. Absolute purity and love wrapped up in one awesome package.

He lived a perfect life, died a horrible death, and experienced a glorious resurrection. He did it all for one reason . . . to redeem us from the bonds of sin and Satan; to rescue us from hell and hopelessness.

Remember the big picture. God created us to be with Him. But we blew it. Our sins separated us from Him. But thank God that is not where the story ends. God sent His own Son to bear the consequences of those countless sins on our behalf. He did it to rekindle that relationship with us once and for all.

HIS HORRIBLE DEATH

Stop for a moment to contemplate the significance of Christ's death on our behalf. Matthew, Mark, and Luke describe the gruesome process that Jesus went through when He suffered for our sins.

After Jesus had been brutally beaten beyond recognition and mocked by a throng of Roman soldiers, He was nailed to a rough, wooden cross. As His body hung naked and twisted, bloodied and bruised for six long hours on the cross, suspended by three nails and His love for you and me, history was being changed forever. For on that cross Jesus was absorbing the judgment of the Father for the sinfulness of all humanity. That's why Jesus screamed in Aramaic, "My God, my God, why have you forsaken me?"

> *"But God demonstrates his own love for us in this: While we were still sinners, Christ died for us."*
>
> **(Romans 5:8)**

THE CHRONICLES OF NARNIA

In the book and movie *The Lion, the Witch and the Wardrobe*, Edmund, the younger brother, makes a deal with the White Witch who rules Narnia, agreeing to betray his brother and sisters for a treat called Turkish Delight. As a result of his sinful choice, tragedy unfolds and the whole of Narnia is threatened with eternal winter under the White Witch's evil rule.

But the great lion Aslan makes the choice to die for Edmund's sin. According to the timeless and eternal laws of Narnia, if somebody sins, they must die for their own transgression, unless somebody innocent chooses to die for their sin instead. After Aslan's horrible death at the hands of the White Witch and her evil minions, Aslan rises from the dead to win the war and destroy the witch.

What a perfect picture of the gospel story! The true "Aslan" is Jesus Christ, the Lion of Judah. Edmund's sin represents Adam's choice to disobey God and betray the whole of humanity, not for a piece of Turkish Delight but for a piece of forbidden fruit. He and all of humanity are condemned to an eternity of dark winter.

But Jesus, the innocent one, makes the choice to die for Adam's sin, for all sin. He, like Aslan, rose from the dead, proving that He was God Himself. In so doing, He destroyed the power of the white witch, Satan himself, forever!

The pain reflected in His scream was not from the gaping wounds in His body but from the fierce, unseen scourge that tore His soul. When Jesus was hanging on the cross, God the Father turned His back on His Son while pouring out His judgment on Him for us.

In that one moment Jesus felt the sting of a trillion hells compressed into one finite moment. He absorbed in full measure the entirety of God's wrath toward the sins of all humanity, including any sin you and I ever committed.

Moments later He declared in triumph the three words of ultimate victory, "IT IS FINISHED!"

The transaction was complete. The price was paid. The sacrifice made. Your sins and mine were obliterated in one sweeping act of God's love and justice.

WHY NOT SOME OTHER WAY?

Why did Jesus have to die? Why couldn't God just snap His fingers and declare us holy? Why did blood have to be shed? The answer is simple: Jesus had to die for us to be able to go to heaven because God is a holy God and demands that every sin is fully punished. Jesus died on the cross because there was no other way for us to be saved. Someone had to die. Either we, the guilty, or He, the innocent. There are no in-betweens with God.

Blood had to be spilled. Hebrews 9:22 tells us that "without the shedding of blood there is no forgiveness." In the Old Testament, an innocent lamb had to be slaughtered in the place of a sinful Jew to satisfy God's righteous demands temporarily. In the new covenant Jesus Christ, the Lamb of God, was sacrificed in our stead to satisfy God's holy requirements

ASHLEY AND THE NONRELIGIOUS JESUS

Ashley had been a Jehovah's Witness as a child but rebelled against her family's belief system as a teenager. It was too narrow and constricting for a wild-hearted teenager filled with hopes and hormones. Although Ashley had been living a lifestyle the last few years that was out of line with her strict upbringing, she had been slowly coming to the realization that something was missing. Her time in God's Word and God's creation during the *GOSPEL Journey Adventure* rekindled a desire in her heart to reconnect with God in a deeper, relational way.

When I began to explain the real, relevant, and nonreligious Jesus, I could see the glimmer of hope in her eyes. She was raised with the religious Jesus, the rules Jesus, the party-pooper Jesus. But now she was hearing about the God who loved her enough to be tortured, mocked, and murdered... for her.

This Jesus was a whole new ball game and Ashley knew it... maybe for the first time.

eternally. As the perfect man, Jesus could die for sinful man. As eternal God, that death payment was infinite.

As difficult as it may be for us to comprehend, the epicenter of our faith is a slaughterhouse where only one lamb was killed . . . the Lamb of God. This historical event was propelled by God's love for us and God's hatred of sin. The significance of that brutal murder 2,000 years ago changed the world forever.

Jesus Christ, the Lion and the Lamb, sacrificed in our place for our sin!

And three days later, He rose from the dead, conquering death and sin once and for all!

✝   ✝   ✝

Now that we are standing at the foot of the rope bridge, we realize it is drenched with the blood of Jesus Himself. It cost Him His life; He built it with His own hands and sanctified it with His own death. The rope bridge is the cross of Christ that spans the gap completely and repairs what Adam and Eve broke.

We stand in awe of how this little bridge could span such an awesome gap.

And now comes the tough part . . . putting our faith in it enough to take the first steps across so that we can complete our journey to the other side.

chapter 13

Everyone Who Trusts In Him Alone Has Eternal Life

The sun is breaking through the clouds, the last patches of fog are burning away and we can see the dazzling mountain sky on the other side of the rope bridge. The beautiful panorama across the chasm stands in stark contrast to the smell of rot and death in our nostrils and the weed-filled landscape that surrounds us. We can't wait to get to the other side. But it's going to take faith in something we've never stood on before. It's going to take stepping off the "safe" ground of our own human efforts and putting our trust in something that somebody else built.

+ + +

THE GOSPEL OF JOHN

The whole book of John was written to unbelievers who needed to understand that the strength of the "rope bridge" was enough to get them to the other side. The book demonstrates how Jesus did miracle after miracle, culminating with the miracle of His

> *"For God so loved the world that he gave his one and only Son, that whoever believes in him shall not perish but have eternal life."*
>
> (John 3:16)

resurrection from the dead, to prove that He was who He claimed to be, the way to a restored relationship with God and eternal life, the rope bridge for everyone who trusts in Him. John 20:31 explains why the book was written: "But these are written that you may believe that Jesus is the Christ, the Son of God, and that by believing you may have life in his name."

Stephén realizes firsthand that faith is required for rock climbing too!

As a matter of fact, the book of John uses the word "believe" 98 times, mostly to describe the way to heaven! Jesus put it this way in John 6:47: "I tell you the truth, he who believes has everlasting life."

The word "believe" here doesn't mean that you just believe that Jesus existed. It actually means "to trust in, to rely upon completely." In other words, to receive the gift of eternal life you must trust in Jesus alone to forgive your sins. It takes more than just believing that He existed; it takes putting your full reliance upon Him to forgive you for all of your sins!

Once you believe in Him you become a child of God forever. John 1:12 tells us, "Yet to all who received him, to those who believed in his name, he gave the right to become children of God."

Not only that, but you are guaranteed eternal life in heaven.

BEN'S BEHAVIOR

Ben was one of the coolest Christians I have ever met. He wasn't forceful with his faith, but he wasn't shy about it either. He would wait for conversations to unfold, whether it was in the hot tub, on the rafting trip, or in the van, and then chime in with a penetrating comment or a great question. He spent so much time listening that when he talked, everybody listened. Sure, there were those who disagreed with Ben, but everyone respected him.

Ben's faith in Jesus was evident in his attitude, his actions, his sly smile, his listening ear, and his caring heart. Ben knew that there was only one way to heaven, through faith in Christ alone, but he never communicated this controversial message in an offensive way. Ben was grace in action, and his grace made a huge impact.

In John 5:24 Jesus said, "I tell you the truth, whoever hears my word and believes him who sent me has eternal life and will not be condemned; he has crossed over from death to life."

Eternal life is not a matter of trying but trusting. Trusting Jesus as your only hope of going to heaven is the most important decision of your life.

What does all this mean for us on the GOSPEL Journey? Simply this: When we put our faith and trust in Christ alone for the forgiveness of sins, we enter into a personal, permanent relationship with God that starts now and lasts an eternity. Moving from the slippery ledge of uncertainty we walk onto a bridge drenched red in the blood of Christ, a bridge that can never break, a bridge that will get us across the chasm of separation between sinful man and holy God, a bridge that is "the way and the truth and the life."

chapter 14

LIFE WITH JESUS STARTS NOW AND LASTS FOREVER

As we make our way across the bridge, we can't help but see the beautiful mountain crest on the other side. It represents our total salvation from sin, our escape from our previously cold, miserable existence when we were surrounded by fear and death. Through Christ's death we have been delivered from the penalty of sin, we are being delivered from the power of sin day after day, and we will be totally delivered from the presence of sin someday when we are with Jesus in heaven, at the highest point of the mountain.

We take our first steps onto this promised land of heavenly hope. The sunshine begins drying out our wet gear and its warmth penetrates deep inside us. But we're not in heaven yet. We have put our faith in Christ, taken the steps across the rope bridge of faith, and received the gift of eternal life. Now we are on a quest toward heaven. We have received eternal life and must walk the pathway of spiritual maturity, growing in our relationship with God every day.

+ + +

QUALITY OF LIFE

Contrary to popular opinion, eternal life doesn't start when you die. It starts as soon as you put your faith in Christ. Jesus put it this way: "Now this is eternal life: that they may know you, the only true God, and Jesus Christ, whom you have sent" (John 17:3).

Take note of what Jesus is saying. The essence of eternal life is a personal relationship with God. It is the quality of this life that Jesus focuses on, not the quantity of it. The beauty of being "saved" is not just what we are saved from, but what we are saved to. We are saved from hell. That's great. I don't want to go there. Neither do you. But we are saved to a beautiful relationship with our

Every cast member brings a different point
of view as they consider the GOSPEL.

brand-new spiritual Daddy, who just happens to be the God of this universe. And that relationship starts the minute we believe.

Realize what this implies. When you trust in Jesus as your Savior you are declared a child of God, you are adopted into relationship with your Creator—that is amazing. You have free access to the very throne room of the King of Kings, because now you are a prince or a princess. You can talk to Him anytime of the day or night, no matter how far you have fallen, no matter where you are or who you are with. He is there, ready, willing, and able to answer you.

Not only can we talk to Him anytime of the day or night, but He can talk to us as well. He has given us 66 love letters that express His mind on everything from relationships to finances to the character of God to the future of humanity. In the pages of Scripture we learn about Him, what He loves, and what He loathes. We discover how to please Him and how to serve Him.

> *"I give them eternal life, and they shall never perish; no one will snatch them out of my hand."*
>
> **(John 10:28)**

Eternal life is a personal relationship with Jesus Christ that just happens to be permanent. It is a two-way street of fellowship and communion where He talks to us and we talk to Him.

QUANTITY OF LIFE

Eternal life is eternal. It never ends. That's a given. That's why it's called eternal life. When we put our faith and trust in Jesus

Christ we are entering a covenant relationship with the God of this universe that can never be broken by us and will never be broken by Him. The blood of Jesus Christ Himself sealed the deal forever.

Jude 24 ensures us that He is "able to keep you from falling and to present you before his glorious presence without fault and with great joy." Here are some verses that show us that eternal life lasts forever:

"All that the Father gives me will come to me, and whoever comes to me I will never drive away. For I have come down from heaven not to do my will but to do the will of him who sent me. And this is the will of him who sent me, that I shall lose none of all that he has given me, but raise them up at the last day." (John 6:37-39)

+

"I give them eternal life, and they shall never perish; no one can snatch them out of my hand." (John 10:28)

+

For I am convinced that neither death nor life, neither angels nor demons, neither the present nor the future, nor any powers, neither height nor depth, nor anything else in all creation, will be able to separate us from the love of God that is in Christ Jesus our Lord. (Romans 8:38-39)

+

Being confident of this, that he who began a good work in you will carry it on to completion until the day of Christ Jesus. (Philippians 1:6)

+

   Therefore he is able to save completely those who come
to God through him, because he always lives to intercede for
them. (Hebrews 7:25)

                                  ✛

   God has said, "Never will I leave you; never will I forsake
you." (Hebrews 13:5)

   Think of it this way. When you were a child and you disobeyed
your dad, did he throw you out of the house for good? Probably not.
He brought you in and gave you a spanking, scolding, or time out.
The same is true of our heavenly Father. When we sin He proves
that He loves us through disciplining us. This heavenly "time
out" could come in many forms of struggles or problems, and
oftentimes it is a direct consequence of our disobedient choices.

TIFFANY'S VOICE

At the very end of the *GOSPEL Journey* reality
series, we all hugged and cried and shared. This
was one wild week. Throughout the week I had
been hearing how beautiful Tiffany's singing
voice was. So I asked Tiffany if she would wrap up the week by
singing a song. With the Rocky Mountains as her backdrop, she
sang the most beautiful live rendition of "On My Knees" that I
have ever heard.

What a beautiful end to our week in the mountains. In many
ways Tiffany's song was a brief glimpse of the power and beauty
of eternal life. When we put our faith in Christ we enter into a
song, a beautiful ballad of hope. The song begins when we put
our faith in Christ, and it never ends. Someday in heaven all our
songs will harmonize as we surround the throne of Christ and
get on our knees to worship our Creator, Redeemer, Lord, and
Friend . . . forever.

God knows how to get our attention and teach us what He desires us to learn.

That's one of the reasons why it's vital that we help new believers understand that when they trust in Christ they are entering into a wonderful relationship with Jesus that is personal, permanent, and unshakeable. This assurance gives new believers the confidence of a secure relationship that can propel them into a lifetime of thankful service to God. Because we must also help them realize that once they come to Christ, the desire to serve Him should flow freely out of gratitude to Him for this amazing gift He has given us.

Once we traverse the rope bridge of Christ and plant our feet firmly on the other side, in one sense, our journey is over. We have crossed the gaping chasm and received the free gift of eternal life. We find ourselves in the midst of breathtaking beauty, gazing in awe at the splendor of our new surroundings. We have entered into an unbreakable, unshakeable relationship with Jesus. We have become a child of God.

In another sense our journey is just beginning. Once we take the last step off the rope bridge, the pathway continues toward the distant crest of the mountain called heaven. Our pack feels lighter, and we move forward with renewed energy. The pathway is our spiritual growth in our newfound relationship with Jesus. Obstacles still creep onto our path, but we discover there are fellow travelers on this same path who are willing to walk alongside us and help us. We must get plugged into relationship with other Christians in a good local church and youth group. We must learn how to study the trail map of God's Word, pray, live in the power of the Spirit, and take others on the GOSPEL Journey.

chapter 15

HOW TO USE THE GOSPEL JOURNEY MESSAGE IN YOUR CONVERSATIONS

So now you understand the whole story of the GOSPEL Journey Message. It's the ultimate love story. It's more than history, it's His story . . . and our story ties right in there along the way.

But how do you take your friends on this exciting journey? How do you explain it to them in a way that they can understand?

While the gospel is a simple message, sometimes sharing it can be a tough undertaking. Many motivated Christian teens don't know what to say. Many informed Christian teens don't care to say it. Hopefully, by now you have the motivation. I just shared with you the information. It's time now to learn the application—how to share the gospel message naturally, in the midst of your relationships.

If you just start quoting the GOSPEL at someone, they may think you are crazy. No one wants to hear someone rattle off a list of theological points and feel like they're being preached at. Conversation, give-and-take dialogue, these are the keys to sharing the gospel relationally with your friends.

USE THE GOSPEL JOURNEY MESSAGE
AS A GUIDE, NOT A SCRIPT

That's why the GOSPEL acrostic is designed to be a conversation guide, not a full script; you write the script in your own words. The six truths in the acrostic are just there in your memory banks to help you make sure you're communicating the whole story of the gospel message. Remember, it's a message, not a method!

Let me give you an example of how the conversation could go. See if you can find each point of the GOSPEL in this conversation. Let's say you are talking to your close friend Jake:

You: Do you ever wonder about God, Jake?

Jake: I don't really know.

You: Well, do you believe in God?

Jake: I guess so.

You: What do you think God wants from you?

Jake: To be a good person...to live a good life, I guess.

You: Yeah, those are good things...but would it surprise you to know that God wants a relationship with you—a relationship that's real here and now, but that also lasts long after you die, that actually lasts forever.

Jake: Come on, man, how do you know what God wants?

You: Well, I base my beliefs about what God wants on what the Bible says. While it's a big, long book, the message God communicates throughout it is really pretty simple. The story of the Bible is that God created us to be with Him. But we humans messed up and ruined our perfect relationship with Him and the rest of the Bible is the story of how He made a way for us to get back into right relationship with Him again.

Jake: Whoa, wait a minute, what do you mean, God created us to be with Him? You mean to tell me that you don't believe in evolution? I mean . . .

You: I'm sure that we could talk about how life began all day. But to be honest, it's not the most crucial thing that you need to understand about the story of Christianity. My point is that God created us to be with Him. His original intent was to pour out His love on all of humanity.

Jake: Well, tell me this then, if God made us to love us, then why is there so much pain and suffering in the world?

You: That's a great question, Jake. And the Bible has a pretty interesting explanation for that very issue and here it is. After God created the first humans, Adam and Eve, to be in relationship with Him, they sinned—that's just another way of saying that they messed up, they missed the mark, they turned away from God. And when they sinned, it impacted the future of all humanity—as a result of the sin of Adam and Eve, death, pain, and suffering entered the world. When that happened, the result was separation from God—we could no longer be in a close, personal relationship with a holy and perfect God.

Jake: So you're saying that all the suffering in the world is not God's fault? It's humanity's fault?

You: That's exactly what I'm saying. We keep Adam and
Eve's sinful legacy going every time we lie, lust,
cheat, or steal. It's all of our faults. But it started
with Adam and Eve. God put them both in a perfect
environment, no sin, no problems, no pain. They
chose to turn their backs on God and they messed
everything up for all of humanity. Because they
cracked humanity's door open to sin, nobody can
meet God's standard of holiness and perfection.

Jake: That seems kind of harsh. God gives up on all of us
because of Adam and Eve's sin.

You: And our own sin.

Jake: It still seems brutal to me.

You: Well, the Bible tells us that God set things up so
that humans have the choice to accept or reject
Him. God doesn't make everybody choose to be in a
relationship with Him. Just like with Adam and Eve,
He gives everybody the choice to turn toward Him in
faith or away from Him in unbelief. And the choice
we make about God reverberates down through all
eternity, meaning that we'll spend eternity with Him
in heaven or eternal separation from Him in hell.

Jake: Well, who wants to go to hell? That's why people try
to live a good life, right? To earn God's favor and go
to heaven and avoid hell. Who wouldn't want to be on
God's good side? No wonder people try to be good!

You: But being in a right relationship with God and going
to heaven is not by being good. As a matter of fact,
the Bible says that sins can never be removed by our
good deeds.

Jake: You mean to tell me that being good doesn't get you into a right relationship with God or get you into heaven?

You: Not even close. The problem is that nobody could be good enough. God is a perfect God and demands perfection of all who dwell in heaven. The Bible makes it clear in Revelation 21:27 that even if you just told one little white lie you could never make it into heaven. To get into heaven we have to be as good as God Himself.

Jake: That seems a little unrealistic, doesn't it?

You: Yes. It is totally unrealistic. It can't be done.

Jake: So is there any good news here in this story of Christianity? Right now it all seems pretty bad to me.

You: Yeah, here is where it starts getting good, really good. Because people can't earn their way to heaven by good deeds, God sent His own Son to become the God-man and live the perfect life that we could never live. Jesus paid the price for our sin by dying on the cross and rising again.

Jake: So you're saying that Jesus Christ died for my sins? Why in the world would God die in my place?"

You: Jesus gave the answer in John 3:16: "For God so loved the world that he gave his one and only Son, that whoever believes in him shall not perish but have eternal life." The answer is because God loves you enough to sacrifice His own Son for your sins.

Jake: So there's nothing I have to do to get to heaven?

If Jesus died for everybody's sin then everybody's going to heaven?

You: No. Jesus said that to have your sins forgiven you must receive what He did for you.

Jake: What does that mean, "receive"?

You: It means you put your faith and trust in Jesus to forgive you for your sins based on what He did for you on the cross. Everyone who trusts in Him alone has eternal life.

Jake: Trusts in Him alone?

You: Yes! He said in John 14:6 that He is the way, the truth, and the life. He said that nobody comes to the heavenly Father except through Him.

Jake: That sounds kind of exclusive and narrow-minded.

You: It is, Jake! Maybe that's why Jesus said that broad is the road that leads to destruction and narrow is the path that leads to eternal life. That narrow path is faith in Jesus alone for salvation. But if you think about it, if Jesus is God and if He loved us enough to die for us on the cross, then He can set the rules of engagement.

Jake: I guess that's the key point—"if Jesus is God." I'm not so sure He is. I think Jesus was a good man.

You: A good man who claimed to be God? Come on, Jake. If He is not God then He is either a liar or a kook. And if He is a kook then I'm one too, for following Him. But if He is God, then He is the way, the only way to a restored relationship with God and eternal life.

Jake: Okay, so let's say I trust in Him. What next?

You: Realize that you can receive the free gift of a life

with God that starts now and lasts forever. Does what I've explained make sense? Is there anything holding you back from putting your faith in Jesus right now?

Jake: I don't know. That's just a lot of stuff to think about. I don't know if I'm ready yet.

You: Well, I'm not trying to force you into a relationship with God, and I understand it's a big deal. In fact, in a lot of ways it's the most important decision you'll ever make. So think about it some and let's continue this conversation in a day or two.

Jake: I can see that it's an important decision...I appreciate your willingness to bring it up with me. Even though, my friend, you really are a Jesus freak.

This "script" is an example of how you can use the GOSPEL Journey as talking point touchstones in the natural ebb and flow of conversation with your friends. Obviously, no two conversations are exactly the same. But this sample will give you an idea of the way a good two-way dialogue between you and a friend could unfold. If you look closely at the dialogue, you can see that each point of the GOSPEL was referred to during the conversation, even though Jake never knew that the acrostic was guiding the interaction.

Maybe it will help you to think of it this way. Learning the GOSPEL acrostic is like putting in the prep work needed to play a guitar. First, you learn the chords. Chords give you the basics you need to be creative and play your own personal, powerful song. In the same way, the GOSPEL acrostic provides you with the basics you need to share the gospel personally and powerfully. By mastering the basics, you can let the Holy Spirit inspire you to engage your friends in genuine, relational, give-and-take conversations.

MEMORIZING THE GOSPEL ACROSTIC

Which raises the dreaded "M-word"—memorization. I wish I had an easier way for you, since memorization is not a popular thing. But I encourage you to memorize the acrostic, word for word because it covers the span of the whole story of the Bible. It covers every major point of the gospel message that a person should know, understand, and accept if he or she is going to become a Christian.

There are other reasons you should memorize these six points, as well. Mastering the GOSPEL will give you confidence as you communicate the message. It will give you key points to discuss along the pathway toward eternal life. It will keep you on track in the conversation.

To review, here are the six truths of the GOSPEL Journey acrostic:

G od created us to be with Him.

O ur sins separate us from God.

S ins cannot be removed by good deeds.

P aying the price for sin, Jesus died and rose again.

E veryone who trusts in Him alone has eternal life.

L ife with Jesus starts now and lasts forever.

EVANGETIPS

How do you memorize something and seal it into your long-term memory? Write down what you are trying to memorize word for word, read it for a minute or two, then five minutes later read it again. In an hour do the same thing again, three hours later do it again, six hours later do it again, and do it one more time before you fall asleep. Repeat this three times a day for the second and third day. Studies show that if you've done that, you will have it sealed in your long-term memory. In other words, it will be hard to forget it. Want to make it easier? Try it with a friend or two or memorize it as a youth group this way. There is power in the tribe.

Once you've memorized the basics, it's time to get creative! Use your own personality and sharing style to approach spiritual conversations with your friends.

THE POWER OF WORD PICTURES

You may also find that using illustrations in the midst of your dialogue with your friends is a powerful way to make your point.

Jesus was a master at using illustrations and word pictures to communicate spiritual truth—that's what His parables are, spiritual word pictures. He used illustrations from the simple farming and fishing lifestyle of His followers: sheep, grain, fig trees and vineyards, to name a few. But you can use illustrations that connect with your life and your friends.

Your illustrations can range from personal ones (like the time you took a leap of faith from a rock cliff into the water below or something else to illustrate faith) to stand-alone illustrations (like the ones I'm about to share with you). The point is that a picture paints a thousand words. I've developed most of the following illustrations after thousands of experiences sharing the gospel. You can choose what fits you best or use your own illustrations to help make the point.

Here are some illustrations you can use to help explain each step of the GOSPEL acrostic:

G od created us to be with Him.

THE ANT PILE

Did you ever know a little kid who loved to take a magnifying glass, put it up to the sky, and use the intensified rays to burn ants in an ant pile (or were you that kid)? Sometimes kids can be cruel. They may laugh but the ants don't think it's funny. Some people view God the same way. They think that He loves to use His magnifying glass to burn people with catastrophes and problems. Nothing could be further from the truth. As a matter of fact, God created us to be with Him. He made the first man and woman to be in perfect relationship with Him in the perfect environment, to pour out His love on them.

O ur sins separate us from God.

THROWING ROCKS AT THE MOON

You could try throwing a rock and hitting the moon, but

you'll never come close. You may throw it farther than me, or anybody on this earth for that matter, but you wouldn't have a chance. The moon is more than 238,000 miles away from the earth. Even if you could throw a rock one mile high you wouldn't even start coming close to having what it takes to hit the moon with a rock.

The same is true with getting into heaven. God's standard for getting into heaven is perfection. We're not even close. You could be the nicest person on the planet and you wouldn't stand a chance of being as good as God. We all miss the mark of God's perfection. By the way, that's what the word "sin" means—"to miss the mark."

S ins cannot be removed by good deeds.

SWIMMING THE OCEAN

Imagine that you and I are standing on the coast of California and we decide to swim to Hawaii. Maybe you make it 15 miles and I make it five or so. It doesn't matter. Because both of us are going to end up on the bottom of the ocean. Why? It is too far for anyone to swim. It is not humanly impossible. In the same way, if we try to make it to heaven by living a good life then we are going to fall way short. Why? According to the Bible we have to be as good as God to get into heaven. Nobody is. So we all miss the mark of God's impossible standard.

WHITE FROSTING/BURNED CAKE

Let's say that I baked you a cake and burned it badly. If I were to cover it in white frosting and give it to you, the cake would still be burned even though you couldn't see it. As soon as you bit into it you would know. Putting white frosting on a burned cake doesn't change the fact that the cake is ruined. Covering our sinful lives with good deeds doesn't change the fact that we have sinned. God sees right through the "frosting" straight to our sin.

P aying the price for sin, Jesus died and rose again.

THE TRUCK

Imagine walking across a busy intersection during rush hour. Suddenly, a speeding truck comes out of nowhere and is heading directly at you. You are not paying close attention and don't see the truck. But someone standing on the corner does. He runs into the street and pushes you out of the way. That person absorbs the full impact of the truck and is killed instantly. This hero took your place in death. He sacrificed his life for yours. In the same way God's anger for sin was headed full speed at you. Christ pushed you out of the way and sacrificed His life so that you could live forever. He died in your place and mine!

E veryone who trusts in Him alone has eternal life.

THE CHAIR

If you trust in a chair then you are willing to sit on it, to put your full weight upon it. If you say that you believe the chair could hold your weight but you're not willing to put your full weight upon it, then you don't have real faith. When it comes to Jesus, it takes more than just believing that Jesus can forgive you for all your sins; it takes putting your full weight upon Him in faith.

Life with Jesus starts now and lasts forever.

THE RIVER
Eternal life is like a river that goes on forever. But this river is just as deep as it is long. You can never reach the end of the river or the bottom of it. It is eternal in both directions. You see, eternal life is more than just living forever, more than an eternal quantity of time. It's deep, an infinite quality of life, a life that will continue forever in an ever-deepening relationship with the God of the universe.

So your spiritual journey with your friends has begun. For some it may be a short journey to Jesus and for others, their road may be longer. Either way, don't give up on your friends. Keep praying for them and pursuing spiritual conversations with them. Remember that somebody didn't give up on you.

BONUS ROUND!

Once you've memorize the 6 key truths of the GOSPEL Journey Message, I strongly encourage you to go for the bonus round and also memorize the 6 key Bible verses found on the next page. They'll provide clear, succinct Biblical backup for you, if the need arises in the midst of your spiritual conversations.

G od created us to be with Him.

Know that the Lord is God. It is he who made us, and we are his (Psalm 100:3a).

O ur sins separate us from God.

For all have sinned and fall short of the glory of God (Romans 3:23).

S ins cannot be removed by good deeds.

All of us have become like one who is unclean, and all our righteous acts are like filthy rags (Isaiah 64:6a).

P aying the price for sin, Jesus died and rose again.

But God demonstrates his own love for us in this: While we were still sinners, Christ died for us (Romans 5:8).

E veryone who trusts in Him alone has eternal life.

For God so loved the world that he gave his one and only Son, that whoever believes in him shall not perish but have eternal life (John 3:16).

L ife with Jesus starts now and lasts forever.

I give them eternal life, and they shall never perish; no one will snatch them out of my hand (John 10:28).

chapter 16

HOW TO PRESENT IT CLEARLY

I don't know what it is with Christians. They love to use terms that confuse the simplicity of the gospel. Even questions like "Are you a Christian?" can be confusing because most people in America think of themselves as Christians in one sense or another. But being born in America doesn't make you a Christian, just as being born in a garage doesn't make you a car.

It is vital as we share the gospel with our friends, teammates, classmates, family members, and neighbors that we are as clear as possible. Here are a few terms to avoid.

1) ARE YOU SAVED?

Saved from what? Saved from boredom or from a fire in the building? Saved from a school bully or a bad teacher?

Replace this term with words everyone can understand, like "Do you know you are going to heaven?" or "Are you sure God has forgiven you for all your sins?"

② LET JESUS INTO YOUR HEART

I'll never forget my Sunday-school teacher challenging us every week during class (after the flannel-graph special-effects show) to "let Jesus into our hearts."

Being the neurotic little kid that I was, I had this mental picture of Jesus desperately trying to squeeze into each ventricle of my heart. Somehow I was unknowingly blocking Him from coming into my heart with some subconscious brain impulse that was impeding my salvation.

But part of my perplexity was my Sunday-school teacher's fault. Although she was doing her best to give the gospel, she was unintentionally confusing me with a term that has been sacredly handed down from generation to generation of traditional American Christians.

③ TURN FROM YOUR SIN

Okay, this is a biggie. I mean, we all want sinners to turn from their sins right? We want them to live a life that pleases God and to rid themselves of their naughty, sinful habits. The problem is, if we are honest, we are still sinners ourselves. When we tell them that they must "turn from their sin" to receive the gift of eternal life, we are asking non-Christians to do something that we are still struggling with ourselves. We are asking them to do something that is an ongoing result of salvation, not a prerequisite to salvation.

Instead we ought to make sure they trust in Christ as their only hope for the forgiveness of their sins first. Once they trust in Christ, their sins are forgiven. They are given the power and desire to turn from their sins. They enter that lifelong struggle of turning from their sins and only fully succeed when they die.

Even the super apostle Paul struggled right up to the end to turn from his sin. Listen to his words to the early Christians:

> For I have the desire to do what is good, but I cannot carry it out. For what I do is not the good I want to do; no, the evil I do not want to do—this I keep on doing. Now if I do what I do not want to do, it is no longer I who do it, but it is sin living in me that does it. (Romans 7:17-20)

If Paul still struggled with turning from his sin and living a life that pleased God, how can we ask an unbeliever, who has no internal capacity to choose what is truly good, to do what we cannot?

Let me give you a real life example of the impact this truth can have in the lives of broken and hurting people. Way back when I was a young, wet-behind-the ears, nineteen-year-old "preacher boy," I had the opportunity to preach at the Denver Rescue Mission. I knew that I had a captive audience. If those men and women wanted to eat and sleep at the rescue mission, they had to listen to my sermon. I also knew that they were used to hearing typical, downtown "turn or burn" sermons. So I decided to try something different.

As I stood behind the pulpit and looked at the room filled with the dysfunctional and the drunk, I noticed that the rescue mission staff was sitting off to my left in some chairs along the wall. They were used to hearing sermons as well. But they weren't prepared for what I was going to say.

"How many of you in this room have ever heard a preacher tell you that if you want to go to heaven, you have to give up your drinking, your smoking, your cussing, your chewing, your drugs, and your sexual immorality?" I asked.

They all kind of looked up at me with groggy looks of acknowledgment. Many raised their hands in affirmation and grunted, "I have."

I went on, "Well, I want to tell you something a little different tonight." I will never forget that moment. Everybody looked up in confusion at once, including the rescue mission staff. "Here's what I want to tell you," I continued. "If you want to go to heaven, keep your alcohol, cigarettes, cuss words, tobacco chew, drugs, and sexual sins." Talk about a cup of coffee to sober up the audience! Their eyes were wide open. Their jaws dropped. By now the rescue mission staff was standing, apparently getting ready to remove me from the pulpit. One of the disheveled men in the audience yelled out a hearty "Amen!"

Now that I had their full attention, I went on, "You keep every single one of your sins, and you come to the cross of Jesus Christ. You simply believe that He died for those sins. You simply place your trust in Him to forgive you for those sins. Not only will He forgive you, but He will come to live inside of you, and He will give you the power and desire to turn from those sins. But you cannot turn from your sins until you have the power to do so. And you cannot have the power to do so until you are forgiven. And you cannot be forgiven until you believe."

The rescue mission staff sat back down. Seven people trusted Jesus that night because of the pure, untainted message of God's grace.[1] And once they trusted Christ, the Holy Spirit came into their lives and began the never-ending process of turning them from their sin!

4 JUST SAY THIS PRAYER

I cringe when I hear Christians use this term with teenagers as a requirement for salvation. Saying "the sinner's prayer" has almost become a magic potion of sorts for some believers. It's almost as though they think that if they can just get somebody to say it, then he or she is saved from sin, death, and hell.

But merely saying a prayer never saved anyone. Jesus never led anybody through the sinner's prayer, and neither did Paul, Peter, nor any of the other apostles. Why? Because there are no magic words that will bring somebody into the family of God. Faith in Christ alone is the only way.

Saying a prayer after the moment of salvation is a great way for the new believer to thank God for the free gift of salvation. But making it a requirement for salvation is a bad idea. I am convinced that there will be many people in hell who said the sinner's prayer. Why? Because they may just have been going through the motions of saying the words without actually putting their faith and trust in Jesus.

PUT YOURSELF IN THEIR SHOES

As you share your faith, always try to remember to put yourself in their shoes. Understanding their point of reference will help you clearly share the gospel message. In other words, some of your friends who have no religious or spiritual background whatsoever may not understand what basic terms like "salvation" or "savior" mean. Maybe instead of "salvation" use the phrase "forgiveness and cleansing from the things we've done wrong." Instead of "savior" use "the one who saves us from our sin." Just be careful and be aware. If you do use a word or term that you sense they don't understand, simply explain what that word or phrase means.

If you aren't sure that your friends understand, ask them if what you are saying makes sense. Take a little extra time to present to them a clear message. When in doubt, spell it out!

chapter 17

HOW TO SHARE YOUR FAITH STORY

When you share the gospel message, it is important to be able to articulate your own story, the story of your personal journey to Jesus. Some people call this a "personal testimony." In a court case, somebody who provides testimony shares what he or she has seen and heard, and what has happened to him or her. In this case, you are sharing what you saw and heard that changed your mind about Christ, and what has happened to you since.

A credible testimony in a court case is hard to deny. It's hard to deny when you're sharing your faith as well. People may be able to argue the facts night and day with you, but it is difficult to deny somebody's personal experience.

The apostle Paul shared his personal story of coming to Jesus in Acts 26 before King Agrippa. It was difficult for this king to deny the authenticity of Paul's story. As a matter of fact, he didn't even try.

The same is true of you and your friends. As you share your story with them, it will be tough for them to say "That's not true!" because you are sharing what you know to be the truth from your own experience.

The challenge is understanding how to share your story in a compelling and authentic way.

SHARING A COMPELLING PERSONAL STORY

A good personal story describing how you came to put your faith in Jesus has three components:

Have you ever seen one of those TV weight-loss commercials? Almost all of them have one thing in common—the Before-and-After Factor. Those television testimonials usually go something like this:

> Here's how I looked before I took Fat-B-Gone [picture of overweight guy without a shirt] and here is how I look now [picture of same guy this time about 100 pounds lighter with firm muscles and tanned skin]. If you use Fat-B-Gone you could look just like me! For only a small investment of $1,000 per bottle your life could be transformed forever. Thanks, Fat-B-Gone!

Can you imagine somebody trying to sell a weight-loss product where the person actually got fatter after taking it? Ridiculous! The whole point of "selling" is making a case for how your life is better after Product X than it was before it. Whether it be weight loss, whiter teeth, better cell service, or faster downloads, selling something to someone else requires that person be convinced that his or her life will be better after using Product X than it was before.

Well, the gospel is not a product, and sharing your faith is not selling—how can you sell something that's free to begin with?—but the same principle applies. There should be a difference in your life after you have experienced Jesus. If not, then why "buy"?

Maybe your personal story goes something like this:

> Before I trusted in Christ I was partying a lot. I came to realize that this was a dead end. To be honest, I got sick of the morning-after guilt. That's when my friend shared Jesus with me and I became a Christian. Since then I haven't been perfect. There have been times I've struggled with my old way of life. But for the most part, I've been seeking to serve Jesus and the morning-after guilt is gone. I have a new reason to party . . . but it's a whole different kind of party.

Or maybe it's more like this:

> I became a Christian when I was a little kid. I don't remember much before then except for the fear that I had in my mind of dying. I think I saw some movie that talked about hell or something and ever since then I was afraid of what was going to happen to me after I died. One day in Sunday school my teacher, Mrs. Johnson, was talking about how we could know for sure we were going to heaven

someday. I was ready to hear it. That day I trusted in Jesus, and ever since then I have had the assurance of knowing I was going to heaven someday.

However your story unfolds, there needs to be a Before-and-After Factor. You need to share how your life has been different since, whether it be stopping the party life or getting assurance of going to heaven someday.

2 THE TURNING POINT

The second key to an effective personal story is sharing the turning point. What was it that helped convince you to believe in Jesus as your only hope for eternal life? Was it the lifestyle of a friend who had something you didn't? Was it a camp message where you realized all that Jesus had endured for you? Was it the feeling of guilt in your heart after doing something you knew you shouldn't have? Was it the fear of death or hell?

Whatever that turning point situation, feeling, or thought was, just realize that it was sent from God to help turn you toward Him.

3 AN AUTHENTIC HONESTY

Nobody's perfect. Have you ever met somebody who thinks he is? Mr. or Miss Perfects tend to make all of us a little nauseated. People don't like to be around plastic people unless they themselves are plastic too.

When it comes to sharing Jesus, don't try to come off as perfect or plastic. Share the story, your story, with grit and raw honesty.

Sure, there should be the primary difference that Jesus made in your life, the Before-and-After Factor, if you will. But you should be willing to share how you've struggled since meeting Jesus too. As a matter of fact, when you think about it, the only difference between you and your unreached friends is that your sins are forgiven and theirs are not. Remember the old quote that describes sharing your faith as one beggar showing another beggar where to find bread.

TIME TO TESTIFY!

Use the space below to write out an account of your personal journey to Jesus. Be sure to include the Before-and-After Factor—what changed in your life since meeting Jesus? Also include the turning point—what was the key person, feeling, or circumstance that led up to your conversion to Jesus? Be sure to be authentic as you share how your life has been since!

Before Factor
Describe how your life was before you met Jesus.

The Turning Point

Describe what led to you becoming a Christian.

After Factor

Describe how your life's been since . . . Be authentic!

A TWO-MINUTE PERSONAL STORY

Now that you have written out your story word for word, it's time to practice it and be able to share it in two minutes or less. Why? Because you never know when it will come in handy! Let's say that you are at a break between classes and you get into a conversation with one of your friends on the way to the next class. Your personal story is a great way to open the door to taking somebody else on the GOSPEL Journey.

Or let's say that you are sharing the gospel with a friend but he or she seems skeptical. That's where you can start sharing your personal story. Again, it's hard to deny somebody's own experience, especially the experience of a close friend.

Okay, you've learned how to take somebody on the GOSPEL Journey. You've discovered how to share your own story. Now it's time to master one of the most difficult parts of sharing your faith—learning to listen. It's time to unlock some of the secrets to having a deep, meaningful two-way dialogue about spiritual truth.

chapter 18

HOW TO USE "SOUL APOLOGETICS"

God gave us two ears and one mouth for a reason, so that we could listen twice as much as we talk. Or so my mom used to say.

Ma was right. Our heavenly Father puts it this way: "My dear brothers, take note of this: Everyone should be quick to listen, slow to speak and slow to become angry" (James 1:19).

In our excitement to share Jesus with those around us, we must learn how to get better and better at listening and discussing without getting angry or argumentative. We must learn to depend on the Spirit of God to give us the strength to keep our mouths shut and our ears open as we encounter other belief systems. It means getting better at asking questions that create open, honest discussion. This works because people usually love talking about themselves. They enjoy sharing their views on life, politics, school, work and, yes, even their religious and spiritual beliefs.

Jesus was especially effective at asking the kinds of questions that probed deeper than the superficial.

- In Matthew 16 Jesus asked Peter, "Who do you say that I am?"
- In Mark 10 Jesus asked the rich young ruler, "Why do you call me good?"
- In Luke 20 Jesus asked the religious leaders of His day why they believed what they believed about who the Messiah would be.

On and on the list of questions Jesus asked those He encountered goes. He asked thought-provoking questions that could trigger authentic dialogue.

Asking good questions is all part of the discussion process. Some questions you ask are for the purpose of learning more about what they believe. Other questions are asked with the intent of causing someone else to think.

TRUE CONFESSIONS

When I first started sharing my faith, it was all one way. I had a message to share and you were going to listen no matter what. I was relentless. Some of that came from my Talker/Stalker mix style of sharing my faith. But most of it came from my personal insecurities and emotional immaturity. I remember that changing somewhat when I met Rod. He was one of those Eastern mystic kind of Kung Fu guys. He was extremely intellectual and self-confident. It took a lot of conversation, prayer, and heated dialogue before he finally became a Christian. In the process I learned how to listen to what was going on in his soul instead of dominating the conversation the whole time. I began to discover how to tap into "soul apologetics" and share in a relational way. To be honest, I'm still learning how to balance being relational and relentless.

KEEP THE DIALOGUE GOING

Earlier in chapter 7 you learned some questions that could help get the conversation started. Here are some open-ended questions that can help keep the dialogue going:

- How did your parents' spiritual beliefs influence you? Do you believe just like them or do you have a different perspective?

- Have you ever been to a church? How did you feel about your experience there? How did it impact your view of Christians?

- Why do you think you hold the views of God that you do now? How have your views changed over the years?

- What do you think about Jesus? Do you think He was the Son of God, a good teacher or something else?

- Why do you think there is so much suffering in the world? Why do you think God would allow it? Do you think God cares about humanity? About you?

- What are your views of the Bible? Have you read it? Do you think it is the Word of God or just some book put together by a bunch of men a long time ago? Why?

The list of possible questions is endless. The point is to ask questions that create open and honest discussion.

And as you seek to deeply listen to somebody else and understand where they're coming from and why, it will prepare you to use an approach I call "soul apologetics." What's that, you may be thinking—it sounds like we're supposed to be apologizing for something. But apologizing is not what apologetics is about at all. Traditional apologetics is about Christians defending their faith through sound, logical arguments, explaining things like why we believe in a Creator, or why we believe in the resurrection. While those are legitimate discussion points, it's not just people's minds that need apologetics. It's their souls as well. Here's how I define it:

Soul Apologetics [sohl*uh-pol-uh-**jet**-iks]. The process of getting to the why behind the lie of what someone is believing and/or how someone is behaving through active listening and dependence on the Holy Spirit.

If we depend on facts to convince somebody of the claims of Christ we are primarily speaking to their intellect. This won't get us very far because in reality, they are spiritually blind and deaf! You can have the best arguments in the world and they will just keep walking by.

When Paul wrote to the believers of Corinth in 2 Corinthians 10:3-5 he addressed this.

"For though we live in the world, we do not wage war as the world does. The weapons we fight with are not the weapons of the world. On the contrary, they have divine power to demolish strongholds. We demolish arguments and every pretension that sets itself up against the knowledge of God, and we take captive every thought to make it obedient to Christ."

In other words, what this passage is saying is that there is a fortress of distorted theology and worldview surrounding unbelievers that we must tear down if we are going to take their thoughts captive for Jesus Christ. How are these strongholds torn down? With spiritual weapons, not earthly arguments!

To go a little further with this analogy, imagine with me that every person out there has some kind of fortress surrounding their soul, keeping it from getting rescued. For some that fortress is small and weak. These individuals are open to hearing the gospel. All you have to do is jiggle the doorknob a few times and it will open. Then you can go in and share the gospel with them and all the reasons to believe and, most likely, they will be open to hearing it and may put their faith in Jesus.

But, for others, there is a true stronghold, complete with moats to cross, hazards to avoid, walls to break down and towers to ascend. You can stand outside of these kinds of strongholds and spout apologetics facts all you want and they will all bounce off them like a rubber ball off a castle wall. No, for these kinds of strongholds, spiritual weaponry must be deployed to break down and break in.

What are some of these weapons? They are the love of Jesus Christ poured out through us, the power of the gospel message, God's Word, intercessory prayer and asking the right kinds of questions.

THE WHY BEHIND THE LIE

"Soul apologetics" is a relational, relentless, spiritual and Socratic approach to apologetics. It is what we see Jesus doing, in one form or another, throughout the gospels. It's what we see Paul doing with the men of Mars Hill in Acts 17. This form of apologetics can be both awkward and effective at the same time. But, if there was a Director of Awkward Moments in the New Testament it was Jesus.

EVANGETIPS

If you're ever been stumped by a difficult question about spiritual things and need some more "traditional apologetics" help finding answers, check out gotquestions.org. You'll find hundreds of questions and answers there on topics ranging from the inspiration of the Bible to the nature of the Trinity.

Jesus was a master at soul apologetics. Throughout the gospels you'll find phrases like: "Jesus, perceiving their thoughts" or "Jesus, knowing their thoughts." He skillfully unlocked *the why behind the lie*. Consider the story of the Samaritan woman at the well in John 4. The lie the Samaritan woman who'd had five husbands believed was "if I just find the right guy, my life will be meaningful and satisfying." Through give and take dialogue, Jesus opened her eyes to the truth that the deepest relational satisfaction is found in a personal relationship with God.

Jesus knew the *lie* and He knew *why* she had bought it because He was God. While we're not God, the Spirit of God dwells in us, and will give us the loving insight we need to help others drill to the core of why they *really* believe what they believe.

Here's an example. Rachel was a student who preferred to pick and choose her beliefs from a vast spiritual menu—much like she might order a Frappe at Starbucks, a bit of this and a bit of that. She was raised in an evangelical Christian church, but she'd come to hate church during her high school years because she'd felt judged there. Her authentic questions were dissed and dismissed. So each week, when her parents made her go to church, she locked herself in the church's bathroom and developed her own belief system. What emerged became her new view of God. She saw God as a black woman who baked cookies (a la *The Matrix*) and reincarnated anyone who couldn't make it into heaven on their first try.

As Rachel shared her story with me, I listened carefully and prayed for insight from the Holy Spirit. Using soul apologetics, I encouraged her to peel back the layers and uncover the why behind the lie of her belief system—the core emotional reasons why someone believes what they believe. In the midst of our conversations, she realized that her rejection of Christianity was rooted in a deep emotional need to reject the judgment she'd felt at church. This realization cracked the door open and allowed her to consider the gospel message with new eyes as she searched for spiritual truth. Eventually, after many conversations with many non-judgmental Christians she put her trust in Jesus.

Once you get behind someone's defensive wall, it can open the door to more challenging questions. One of my favorites is: "Have you ever considered the possibility that you might be wrong about what you believe?"

"WHAT IF YOU'RE WRONG?"

Asking your non-believing friends the question "What if you're wrong?" forces them to consider the eternal implications of being wrong about who Jesus is and how eternal life is obtained. Across my years of faith-sharing, I've seen this question work powerfully. But the most impact I've ever seen it have was with a lady named Lynn.

When I broached the topic of Christianity with Lynn she began to hammer me with question after question. Questions like:

- Do you believe that Jesus is the only way to heaven?
- What about the Jews, Hindus, and Muslims?
- What happens to those who reject Jesus?

I responded with the classic apologetic arguments from one of the great Christian thinkers of the twentieth century, C. S. Lewis. I explained to her that Jesus is either Lord, lunatic, or liar because He claimed again and again to be God in the flesh. From the hundreds of prophesies about Jesus that were completely fulfilled, to the weight of eyewitness testimony, I stacked the evidence of Christ's deity before her. She didn't blink.

"I believe that as long as you are sincere you will be okay," she replied.

"What about Hitler? He was sincere," I shot back.

Again, she was cemented firmly in her convictions that my conclusions were too "narrow-minded." After several minutes of loaded discussion, I realized that I was getting nowhere.

 EVANGETIPS

Be careful. A surgeon doesn't use only a scalpel. A good surgeon uses clamps, clips, sponges, and an assortment of other surgical instruments. The scalpel is used to make cuts; a lot of the rest of the instruments are used to stop the bleeding. Make sure you use this question appropriately as you cut into another person's belief system, and use a lot of love and listening skills to help stop the bleeding.

Although we were talking about some pretty intense subjects, neither of us raised our voice. This was an authentic dialogue and didn't have a hint of mean-spiritedness.

So I decided to ask her the question. "Lynn, let me ask you one thing. What if you are wrong?"

"What do you mean?" she asked hesitantly.

"What if you are wrong?" I continued. "What if there is a real heaven, a real hell, and a real Jesus whom you are rejecting as your only hope of heaven? What if when you die you stand before His throne and have to give an account of why you didn't believe? What if all your conclusions about who goes to heaven are wrong and what the Bible says is right?"

"I'm not wrong!" she defiantly proclaimed.

I continued, "Lynn, you told me yourself that you were an 'open-minded liberal' and that I was a 'close-minded Christian.' So if you are open-minded you must at the very least consider the possibility of your being wrong about this, otherwise you are not open-minded, you're just a liberal . . . and a close-minded one at that."

Her mouth dropped wide open. Up until then she had a comeback for every shred of evidence I laid before her. This time she had no snappy comeback. I must commend her for her honesty. She looked in my eyes and said, "What if I am wrong? I have never even thought about that possibility! What a good question! If I'm wrong then I am going to hell!"

A short time later I saw Lynn talking to her husband. I was close enough to overhear her say, "Honey, what if we are wrong about all this stuff that we believe?" Seeds of doubt were sown in the hope that the flower of faith would soon sprout, bloom, and transform.

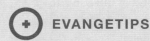 **EVANGETIPS**

Check out the book *Shreddin the Gnar* to learn more about soul apologetics. *Shreddin* captures a candid conversation between my friend, Zane Black, and me as we discuss how to talk to people about God with love and respect. It's packed with practical insights that will challenge and equip you to dive into deep, radical spiritual conversations with your friends. Pick up a copy at www.dare2share.org/store.

ASK-LISTEN-TELL

As you engage non-believers in spiritual conversations, try using soul apologetics. It will help you **ask** the hard questions, **listen** insightfully and then **tell** them about the gospel message in a loving way that speaks uniquely into others' hearts and lives. Often when people block God out of their lives, it's because something is pulling them in a different direction—a hurt in the past, a perception of how things ought to be, a desire to be self-sufficient, or an unwillingness to acknowledge failure, to name a few.

Believe me, the old adage is true, "You'll never argue somebody into the kingdom of God." But the Word of God, the Spirit of God and the gospel of Christ will do their work in others' hearts as you share with a loving heart and two listening ears. When you do that in His strength and not your own, He will give you the wisdom you need to love, listen and share Jesus with others.

Check out this verses that remind us of the importance of depending on the Spirit in this process:

"But when they arrest you, do not worry about what to say or how to say it. At that time you will be given what to say, for it will not be you speaking, but the Spirit of your Father speaking through you." (Matthew 10:19-20)

As you trust in the Spirit of God He will guide you in what to say as you share with your friend the greatest message on planet earth. Depend on Him!

SHARING IN LOVE

When you love people, listen to them and engage in genuine interactive sharing with them, you begin to have meaningful communication. In this dialogue the gospel message is unleashed and begins to reach them at the deepest level. You get past petty excuses and little arguments and get to the core of their soul.

Keep in mind that you should never think of your friends, classmates, teammates, neighbors, family members, and coworkers as projects; they are people—people who desperately need the hope of Jesus. Our hearts need to be broken for them.

We must be controlled by the Holy Spirit. The first fruit He produces through us is love, according to Galatians 5:22. So if you are not loving the person as you share Jesus, you are operating in your own strength. And guess what? You are not strong enough to save a soul on your own.

We must love everyone we encounter with the affection of God Himself. Our hearts should be broken over their current spiritual condition and their future eternal destination. We should care about them, their lives, their hurts, and their questions. One of the greatest evangelists who ever lived put it this way:

> If I speak in the tongues of men and of angels, but have not love, I am only a resounding gong or a clanging cymbal. If I have the gift of prophecy and can fathom all mysteries and all knowledge, and if I have a faith that can move mountains, but have not love, I am nothing. If I give all I possess to the poor and surrender my body to the flames, but have not love, I gain nothing. (1 Corinthians 13:1-3)

Without love we gain nothing, we do nothing, we are nothing. Love is the ultimate description of Christianity and should be our defining characteristic as representatives of the Lord Jesus.

Some famous verses in the 1 Corinthians 13 "love" passage describe how we should lovingly share Jesus with others:

> Love is patient, love is kind. It does not envy, it does not boast, it is not proud. It is not rude, it is not self-seeking, it is not easily angered, it keeps no record of wrongs. Love does not delight in evil but rejoices with the truth. It always protects, always trusts, always hopes, always perseveres. Love never fails. (verses 4-8)

Think about what this means for you as you share Jesus with those God brings across your path. We never have a right to be rude, impatient, angry, or arrogant. Instead we should be selfless, trusting, hopeful, positive, and persistent.

This kind of love is hard to resist.

So before you begin to share Jesus with those around you, take a look at the inside of your heart. Make sure that the stuff propelling you to share Jesus is love and not some other lesser thing.

CONSTANTLY IMPROVE

Learning how to use soul apologetics and how to love in the power of the Holy Spirit doesn't happen overnight. It is an ongoing process. Be patient. Don't give up. Keep trying to love, listen, ask questions, share the truth, refuse to argue and ask God to guide you.

Believe me, I'm still learning myself.

CAN I GET A WITNESS?

I'm Elizabeth. I'm 16 and from Colorado. I've talked to most of my friends about God. It's amazing because most of my friends are actually interested in talking about spiritual things. They aren't interested in the "I'm right, your wrong" approach but they are interested in thinking and talking about the meaning of life and philosophical ideas. My friends are more receptive when I engage them in a discussion instead of us trying to prove each other wrong. When I ask my friends questions, they genuinely think about their views and question them instead of just dismissing God.

chapter 19

HOW TO INVITE SOMEONE INTO A RELATIONSHIP WITH CHRIST

Okay, you've launched into a spiritual conversation with your friend and shared the gospel. You've been relational. What do you do now? You've become lovingly relentless as you encourage him or her to consider Jesus. You can do this by asking him or her a few simple questions:

- Does what we've talked about make sense? Do you understand that God wants a relationship with you that starts now and lasts forever? (If it didn't make sense, go over it again, maybe using some more of the illustrations you learned in chapter 15. If it did make sense, then move on to the next question.)

- Is there anything holding you back from putting your faith in Jesus right now?

While bringing up the gospel with your friends may be the most uncomfortable part of sharing the gospel, this last question is a close second. Why? It puts them on the spot. It causes them to verbalize whether or not they will accept or reject Jesus as the one who will save them from their sins.

Why is this important? Because, quite honestly, if they don't trust in Christ today and they die tomorrow, then they will be separated from God in hell forever. Maybe that's why the apostle Peter pushed his listeners so hard to come to Christ right away in Acts 2:40: "With many other words he warned them; and he pleaded with them, 'Save yourselves from this corrupt generation.'"

Maybe that's why God reminds us in 2 Corinthians 6:2, "I tell you, now is the time of God's favor, now is the day of salvation." There's no better time than today to trust in Christ as your only hope of forgiveness, because there's no guarantee of tomorrow.

As you seek to invite your friend into a relationship with Christ, remember Jesus' Parable of the Sower! Here are the words of Jesus in Mark 4:3-9:

"Listen! A farmer went out to sow his seed. As he was scattering the seed, some fell along the path, and the birds came and ate it up. Some fell on rocky places, where it did not have much soil. It sprang up quickly, because the soil was shallow. But when the sun came up, the plants were scorched, and they withered because they had no root. Other seed fell among thorns, which grew up and choked the plants, so that they did not bear grain. Still other seed fell on good soil. It came up, grew and produced a crop, multiplying thirty, sixty, or even a hundred times." Then Jesus said, "He who has ears to hear, let him hear."

Jesus is reminding His disciples here that not all of those they share the message with will respond with a "Yes, I believe!"

He goes on to explain that some who hear the message will have the message scavenged by Satan. Others will seem to accept it but will have no spiritual roots and fizzle out or be choked by the weeds of worldliness. But some seeds they sow will fall on fertile ground and multiply. What's the Evangetips here? Don't get discouraged if not everybody responds positively to the gospel message! Go with the growers and pray for the others! Keep sharing and keep asking them to respond.

WARNING!

As you share the gospel, remember that for some people coming to Christ will be a short trip, and for others it will be a long journey. Some of your friends may respond right away to the gospel. Others may take a while to come around. Never give up! It took 12 years of praying and a case of life-threatening cancer to finally convince my Uncle Richard to trust in Christ as his Savior. I started sharing the gospel with him when I was 15 years old. He finally came to Christ when I was 27. Within a few months, he was in heaven. It was worth every conversation, every prayer, every sleepless night. I can't wait to see him someday. Don't give up on your friends who are on the longer journey to Jesus!

FISHING WITHOUT REELING

I was raised in a fisherman's home. My grandpa was a fisherman. He took me fishing a lot when I was a kid. He taught me how to bait the hook, cast the line, wait for the bite, set the hook into the fish's jaw with a flick of the wrist, and then reel it in. I can't imagine him telling me to go through all of the hassle of catching the fish without reeling it in after it bites.

Although fishing is kind of a crude analogy to sharing

one's faith (but don't be mad at me . . . Jesus started it!), I think the point is strong. When we bait the hook by sparking people's interest in spiritual things, then set the hook by sharing the gospel with them, it only makes sense to reel them into the family of God by asking them the right questions after they hear the message.

So be relentless about helping your friends reach a decision about trusting in Jesus by asking them a few key questions. And if they do decide to trust in Jesus, you can gently guide them into a prayer of thanksgiving that will help them express their gratitude to Jesus for what He has done for them.

A PRAYER OF THANKSGIVING

Though merely saying a prayer never saved anybody from sin, leading others in prayer is a great way to help those who have put their faith in Christ for the first time to thank God for the free gift they just received. If you lead somebody through a prayer, make sure they know that saying the prayer doesn't get them right with God; rather, it's simply a way for them to thank God for the free gift they just received through faith. The prayer should be short, simple, and clear. Maybe something like this:

> Dear God, thank You so much for forgiving all my sins through Jesus Christ. Through His death my sins are forgiven. Through His resurrection I have new life. Now that I have been forgiven, teach me to live a life that pleases You, not because I have to in order to get to heaven, but because I'm thankful that I am going to heaven. Amen.

Today is the day of salvation!

chapter 20

HOW TO MAKE A PLAN
FOR SHARING YOUR FAITH

You've learned the basics of sharing your faith and you're committed to THE Cause of making disciples who make disciples. You're determined to step up and share your faith in your own unique way and you know how to invite someone to have a personal relationship with Christ. But you have lots of friends who need Jesus and reaching them all feels overwhelming. Where do you start? How do you hold yourself accountable and stay purposeful about reaching out?

THE CAUSE CIRCLE

There's a simple tool that can help. It's called THE Cause Circle and it breaks out the process of sharing your faith into 3 essential steps: 1) PRAY: pray for your friends, 2) PURSUE: bring God up in conversations and 3) PERSUADE: actively work to convince them that Jesus is the way.

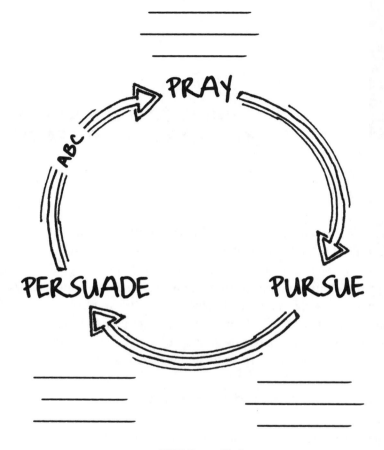

THE Cause Circle

Using THE Cause Circle will help you identify which friends you intend to start sharing your faith with. In the center of the circle, write the names of all your friends who need Jesus. Then identify 3 friends you want to begin praying for regularly and enter their names in the "Pray" section of the circle.

EVANGETIPS

You can download a free copy of THE Cause Circle from Dare 2 Share's website. Go to www.dare2share.org/thecause/the-cause-circle/. Print it out, fill it out and be purposeful about praying, pursuing and persuading!

PRAY

Sharing your faith all starts with prayer! Scripture lays this truth out for us in the following key verses:

> My [Jesus'] prayer is not for them alone. I pray also for those who will believe in me through their message, that all of them may be one, Father, just as you are in me and I am in you. May they also be in us so that the world may believe that you have sent me. (John 17:20-21)
>
> +
>
> Devote yourselves to prayer, being watchful and thankful. And pray for us, too, that God may open a door for our message. (Colossians 4:2-3)

Prayer changes things and opens doors for Jesus' message of grace and forgiveness!

But prayer not only prepares other's hearts for the gospel, it also prepares you. It will keep you connected to God's heart for the lost and it will help you tap into God's wisdom. James 12:5 says: "If any of you lacks wisdom, he should ask God, who gives generously to all without finding fault, and it will be given to him."

Pray regularly that God will provide you His wisdom so you can share your faith in a clear and compelling way.

PURSUE

Once you begin praying for your friends, I'm confident that your "God-talk radar" will become more sensitive and you'll begin to spot opportunities to bring God up in your conversations. When that happens, move your friend's name to the "Pursue" section of the circle. Then go back and add a new name to the "Pray" section.

The "Pursue" and "Persuade" stages of THE Cause Circle are your opportunity to apply all the things you've learned in the rest of this book! For example, watch for the fork in the road in your conversations and use opening questions and natural transition to talk about spiritual things.

In the "Pursue" stage of sharing your faith, you'll need to be sensitive, but insistent. It's natural to talk about the things you love and are passionate about, so tap into your passion fuel and let your love for Jesus overflow into your day-to-day conversations with others.

PERSUADE

When your spiritual discussions begin to move deeper, you've hit the "Persuade" stage of THE Cause Circle.

⊕ EVANGETIPS

There's something powerful about a life of doing good deeds for other people. When Mother Teresa was alive, she had earned the respect of the entire planet because of her lifelong sacrificial work in the streets of Calcutta, India. When you are always doing things for others, you too will earn a reputation throughout your school as someone who loves God and loves others. This reputation can open up the door for you to share Jesus in a powerful way.

Scripture says, "Neither do people light a lamp and put it under a bowl. Instead they put it on its stand, and it gives light to everyone in the house. In the same way, let your light shine before men, that they may see your good deeds and praise your Father in heaven" (Matthew 5:15-16). Here are some ideas that can get you started doing some good deeds:

- Buy lunch for someone you don't know (or do know but don't hang with) at school
- Write notes of encouragement to those who seem down
- Help others with their homework
- Take time to listen
- Sit with somebody during lunch you don't know well and get to know him or her
- Coordinate a school-wide canned food drive for a local rescue mission
- Coordinate a neighborhood cleanup
- Get a group of teenagers from your school to visit a retirement center on a Saturday just to talk to the elderly and to encourage them.

The list of possibilities is almost endless. The point is to start living a life of good deeds and let your little light shine!

In Greek (the original language of the New Testament), the word persuade is *peitho*. *Peitho* is used 8 times in the New Testament in connection with evangelism. Here are a couple examples:

> Every Sabbath he reasoned in the synagogue, trying to persuade Jews and Greeks. (Acts 18:4)

+

> Then Agrippa said to Paul, "Do you think that in such a short time you can persuade me to be a Christian?" Paul replied, "Short time or long—I pray God that not only you but all who are listening to me today may become what I am, except for these chains." (Acts 26:28-29)

It's in this phase of your faith-sharing efforts that you'll find it's essential to be able to explain the message of the gospel in a clear and compelling way.

Don't be afraid to tap into the persuasive power of Scripture in this stage of your conversations. The following two passages make it crystal clear that there is something internally powerful about God's Word. It is sharp like a knife. When we listen to it, it can cut deeply into our consciences and expose us for what we really are. And it always accomplishes its goal, whether it be conviction or conversion.

> For the word of God is living and active. Sharper than any double-edged sword, it penetrates even to dividing soul and spirit, joints and marrow; it judges the thoughts and attitudes of the heart. Nothing in all creation is hidden from God's sight. Everything is uncovered and laid bare before the

eyes of him to whom we must give account.
(Hebrews 4:12-13)

+

So is my word that goes out from my mouth: It will not
return to me empty, but will accomplish what I desire and
achieve the purpose for which I sent it. (Isaiah 55:11)

What does this mean for you as you work to persuade your
friends to consider Christ? Simply this: As you share the gospel
with others, it can help to use verses from the Bible. In addition
to the verses found at the end of Chapter 15 that I challenged you
to memorize. Here are a few more easy-to-memorize verses that
I think every Christian teenager should know by heart:

"I tell you the truth, he who believes has everlasting life."
(John 6:47)

+

"And I will ask the Father, and he will give you another
Counselor to be with you forever." (John 14:16)

+

The wages of sin is death, but the gift of God is eternal
life in Christ Jesus our Lord. (Romans 6:23)

+

For it is by grace you have been saved, through faith—and
this not from yourselves, it is the gift of God—not by works,
so that no one can boast. (Ephesians 2:8-9)

+

He saved us, not because of righteous things we had done, but because of his mercy. He saved us through the washing of rebirth and renewal by the Holy Spirit. (Titus 3:5)

Memorizing these verses will give you some useful truths from God's Word to pick from when you are discussing spiritual things with your friends. For help on how to memorize, reread the "Evangetips" section in chapter 15.

Remember that the "persuade" stage of THE Cause Circle is designed to help you stay focused and purposeful as you share Jesus with others. Seeking to persuade your friends doesn't mean you turn into a pit bull and arm twist them into belief. No, your goal is to lovingly do all you can to get them to give Jesus a serious look.

WARNING!

Don't fall into the trap of thinking that you're offering your friends just one more option among equally valid belief systems. The gospel is not just another idea. It is the greatest story ever told. The power of this message is not philosophical speculation or another religion. It is far from either. It is the truth. So share this message in humble confidence knowing that it is the truth.

What exactly are you trying to lovingly persuade your friends to do? I think of it as the ABCs of disciple making:

- **A**ccept Christ
- **B**elong to a church
- **C**ommit to THE Cause

These ABCs represent the core essentials of what it will take to effectively make disciples who make disciples! You'll learn more about each of them in the next chapter, so read on!

chapter 21

HOW TO HELP NEW
BELIEVERS LIVE THE CAUSE

In Matthew 28:19-20 Jesus tells us to "go and make disciples...
teaching them to obey everything I have commanded you." We're
not just to be about bringing people into a relationship with God.
Our job also includes helping them become disciples who make
disciples.

How do we do that? I believe the Bible points to three core
essentials—what I call the ABCs of making disciples.

A – ACCEPT CHRIST

When someone puts their faith and trust in Jesus Christ, it is
an absolute miracle. They are transformed and transferred—
transformed from a child of the devil (John 8:44) to a child of
God (John 1:12) and transferred out of the kingdom of darkness
into the kingdom of God (Colossians 1:13).

You have helped them take a huge step of eternal
significance, but your job's not done yet. Now it's time to help
them grow in their relationship with Jesus.

B – BELONG TO A CHURCH

How do you do that? You encourage them to get plugged into a local church and you help them get trained in the basics of living their newfound faith!

Can you imagine a doctor bringing a newborn baby into this world, cleaning it off, wrapping it in a warm blanket, and then throwing it into a trash can? Of course not! The baby is kept warm, clean, and fed. The goal is that the brand-new baby grows with just the right amount of rest and nutrition and love.

What's true of newborn babies in the earthly realm is true in the spiritual realm as well. When we were "born again" into the family of God, we needed every bit as much warmth and nutrition and love as a new baby does. The reason you are reading this book to begin with is because somebody took care of you after you became a child of God and helped you grow into a healthy, thriving Christian.

So how do you help newborn babies in Jesus grow into spiritually developed believers? There are three things we need to give them: shelter, nutrition, and lots and lots of love.

 **SHELTER**

More than anything a new believer needs shelter. This is a warm place where he or she can grow and thrive. What is it for a new believer? It is a local church! This incubator of care is where the newborn believers find the warmth and security they need to grow spiritually. If you have the privilege of bringing somebody into the kingdom of God, take him or her to church and youth

EVANGETIPS

Dare 2 Share Ministries has developed numerous resource for new and growing believers. Go to dare2share.org and use the free weekly resource called "Soul Fuel" which tackles the core truths of Christianity in a real, relevant, and teen-friendly way. Alert your youth leader to the accompanying resources for them to use as well. Or download the discipling resource *Now Grow!* from www.dare2share.org/store. It's a great, inexpensive resource for helping new believers get grounded in their faith and, in turn, become disciples who make disciples.

group with you! Without church, new believers could spiritually freeze and die.

NUTRITION

When somebody comes into the family of God they need the spiritual food that is going to help them grow into healthy Christians. This nutrition comes from the Bible. It is the basic stuff of Christianity. Answers to questions like who God is, why the Bible can be trusted, and what prayer is are all-important in the basic nutrition package.

When a newborn baby comes into the world the most basic nutrition is received almost exclusively from his or her mother's milk. This milk provides nutrients to help the baby get strong and enzymes to prevent sickness and disease in those crucial early months. In the same way, the Bible describes itself as this kind of mother's milk for every believer: "Like newborn babies, crave pure spiritual milk, so that by it you may grow up in your salvation, now that you have tasted that the Lord is good" (1 Peter 2:2-3). So help your new believer get grounded in the Word of God.

CAN I GET A WITNESS?

My name is Vanessa and I'm from Boulder, Colorado. If I could describe my life in one word before I met Christ, it would be: Chaos. Ultimately, I gave in to just about every peer pressure you can think of… and for what? Nothing ever satisfied. I knew about Jesus growing up in a Christian family, but outside of your basic bible story, my concept of Him was more like my concept of Elvis (real, a self-declared king, but in the end just a man).

Desperate for something to make sense of my life, I asked everyone I knew (and I do mean everyone) what his or her thoughts were about God. Finally fed up with getting my questions diverted face-to-face, I sought out the next best thing. Facebook. I ended up sending a message to one of my teachers from elementary school, whose profile clearly exclaimed her faith in God. We ended up meeting for coffee, and talking… and a week later, Debbie and her husband, Greg, led me into a relationship with Jesus.

From the moment when I finally saw the Truth, I wanted to tell everyone! My friends, family, people on the bus and at the grocery store, were all at risk of being "gospelized." The first thing I did was to make a list of people I wanted to share the gospel with, and number one on that list was my best friend. She was one of the first people I told of my life changing experience, and that first conversation led to another, which led to yet another. It wasn't long before she put her faith and trust in Jesus. After that she jumped on board the same faith-sharing journey I am on, and began telling everyone about Jesus, even her ex-boyfriend! He came to church with us one week, and though he isn't ready yet… he is on both of our lists.

(3) LOTS AND LOTS OF LOVE

Love is the warm blanket that wraps these newborn babies. It is the tender, loving care of spiritual fathers and mothers who look after, rock, kiss, and hold the newborn. It's how Paul loved new believers. He writes to them, "We were gentle among you, like a mother caring for her little children. We loved you so much that we were delighted to share with you not only the gospel of God but our lives as well, because you had become so dear to us" (1 Thessalonians 2:7-8).

How do we love new believers? We serve them. We listen to them. We help them learn to take those first few steps of obedience from baptism to discovering their very own spiritual gifts. In this whole exciting process we must be patient and somewhat pushy at the same time. We love them enough to accept them as they are, but we also love them enough not to leave them there.

Just as any baby goes through different phases of development, from being able to roll over to learning to crawl and then walk, new believers must be encouraged to make spiritual progress as well. We are there like a mom and dad encouraging them to take that next step, picking them up when they fall and cheering them on again.

C – COMMIT TO THE CAUSE

New believers are usually brimming with excitement about their newfound relationship with Jesus. What better time to tap into their natural desire to share with everyone around them the amazing news that God longs to be in a relationship with every single person on the planet? Your role is to help

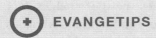

EVANGETIPS

When it comes to convincing new believers of the importance of not only attending church but also serving Christ with all of their hearts, I have found "The Million-Dollar Question" to be very useful.

Once someone indicates faith in Jesus and I am convinced that they understood the gospel message, I use this powerful question, "If I were to give you a million dollars right now, would you slap me and walk away?" Their answer usually goes something like, "Of course not." When I probe a little deeper and ask why, they answer something like, "Because I am grateful for your tremendous gift!" Then I ask them another question, "God has just given you something of infinitely more value than a million dollars. He has given you eternal life! Are you going to slap Him in the face and walk away or are you going to serve Him?" Every time their answer is "serve Him." "Why?" I ask. "Because I am grateful for His tremendous gift to me" is usually their response.

The power of The Million Dollar Question is that it enables the new believer to understand that the reason we serve Jesus Christ is not a "have to" but a "want to." We serve Jesus not to prove, keep, or earn our salvation but because of it! Wholehearted service to God flows out of a thankful heart. The Million Dollar Question helps new believers get started with just that!

and encourage them as they begin to share their new faith with their friends.

Sharing our faith isn't something that should wait until later, until our walk with God is polished and perfected. It should start just as soon as someone understands the message of the gospel! Of course there are things you can do to help them as they learn to share their faith. Give them this book to read. Pray for them. Pray with them for their unreached friends. Challenge them. Encourage them. Help them find answers to any questions that arise out of their conversations with others.

Do your best to follow up every single person you bring to Jesus. Get these newborns plugged into a church where they can get the food, shelter, and love they need. And get them committed to THE Cause of making disciples who make disciples.

chapter 22

HOW TO STAND AGAINST THE EVIL ONE

When you choose to commit to THE Cause and share your faith, especially if you do it drenched in the Holy Spirit's power, beware. The kingdom of darkness will muster its evil powers on a quest to defeat your efforts. So don't underestimate Satan and his army of fallen angels who will do everything in their power to get you to quit. It's important to understand your enemy and some of the strategies he may deploy to get you sidetracked.

The evil one and his army of fallen angels will attempt to destroy. If they can't, they will, at the very least, try to deceive, distract, and discourage you.

How? They'll whisper in your ear things like, "Hey, don't go pushing your religion on your friends. Build the relationship a little bit longer before you bring it up. And by the way, you have some areas in your life that need to be corrected before you go out and share Jesus. Just wait. It will all work out in God's perfect timing." Shut those whispers down, remember to balance relational and relentless and pray for God's perfect timing.

TRUE CONFESSIONS

I went through a time in my life where I rebelled against living THE Cause out loud. I bought the lies of Satan that if I just lived a godly life in front of other teenagers they would see it, ask me about it, and trust in Christ. After months of trying this I realized that nobody was noticing, nobody was asking, nobody was coming to Christ. So I started bringing Jesus up again while still seeking to live a life that backed up my message. What I realized is that it is not either/or, either sharing Jesus with my life or with my lips. It took both/and, both living the message and sharing it in a relational and relentless way.

If that doesn't work they'll distract you with sports, work, hobbies, relationships, studies—anything and everything. They'll do their best to keep you so busy that you forget people need Jesus—that without Him they are "harassed and helpless, like sheep without a shepherd" (Matthew 9:36).

These demonic entities may lie to you with thoughts like, *"Are you even sure about this whole thing called Christianity yourself? I mean, come on, you are putting your faith in a man you've never met, who lived, died, and supposedly rose from the dead two thousand years ago. You are staking your eternal destiny on some dude named Jesus who claimed to be some kind of God-man. You better be sure yourself before you try pushing this wacky belief on somebody else."*

Maybe what they'll do is discourage you. They'll remind you of your less-than-perfect home life or the fact that you don't have a boyfriend or girlfriend. Perhaps they will whisper lies in your ears when you step on the scale or look in the mirror. They'll try to tell you you're too fat, too ugly, too skinny, too zitty, too whatever.

Don't buy the lies.

Demons are just doing what they do. Their purpose is to sidetrack the divine plan of advancing the kingdom of God through His children. If our purpose is to glorify God, their purpose is to "de-glorify" Him. The last thing Satan and his army wants is for your friends, classmates, teammates, and neighbors to come to Christ.

WHO IS SATAN?

Satan is a real being. He was created by God to be an angel—as a matter of fact, the top angel of God. Here's how God describes him, as told by the prophet Ezekiel:

> "You were the model of perfection,
>> full of wisdom and perfect in beauty.
> You were in Eden,
>> the garden of God;
> every precious stone adorned you:
>> ruby, topaz and emerald,
>> chrysolite, onyx and jasper,
>> sapphire, turquoise and beryl.
> Your settings and mountings were made of gold;
>> on the day you were created they were prepared.
> You were anointed as a guardian cherub,
>> for so I ordained you.
> You were on the holy mount of God;
>> you walked among the fiery stones.
> You were blameless in your ways
>> from the day you were created
>> till wickedness was found in you." (Ezekiel 28:12-15)

The devil was created to be God's personal bodyguard (why He would need one, I don't know!). He was perfect in wisdom, beautiful to look at, and indescribably powerful. He had it all—a big bench press, a high IQ, and a dazzling smile. And maybe that was the problem. At some point maybe he caught a glimpse of himself in a golden heavenly mirror. Moments later he was posing and flexing and thinking, "You are one handsome, strong, and smart dude. If you applied yourself, you could climb the corporate ladder here in heaven. As a matter of fact, I bet the angels in heaven would follow you and you could completely take over this place. All you have to do is dethrone the Son of God."

Whatever the exact conversation that Satan had with himself was, he convinced himself that he could plan a mutiny among the angels that would end up with his ruling and Jesus looking for a new job. Here's how the book of Isaiah describes what happened:

> You said in your heart,
>> "I will ascend to heaven;
> I will raise my throne
>> above the stars of God;
> I will sit enthroned on the mount of assembly,
>> on the utmost heights of the sacred mountain.
> I will ascend above the tops of the clouds;
>> I will make myself like the Most High."
> But you are brought down to the grave,
>> to the depths of the pit. (Isaiah 14:13-15)

The devil gathered a third of the angels to help him take over heaven. He launched his short-lived mutiny. Suffice it to say that instead of ruling in heaven he and all of his fellow rebels got thrown out. Now these invisible enemies roam and comb the earth, seeking to use mankind to carry the mutiny on every day.

Their biggest victories come when they keep God's children (that's you and me) from living and sharing our faith. Believe me, they are working overtime to keep your life and your mouth self-centered and quiet about Jesus.

HOW DO WE DEFEAT THE DEVIL?

James 4:7 tells us how to defeat the devil every time and anytime he attacks: "Submit yourselves, then, to God. Resist the devil, and he will flee from you."

There is a two-step process you must go through to win against him. First of all, submit to God. Choose to put yourself under God's full command; surrender to Him with all of your heart. It's when you choose to do this that you are filled with the power that comes from the Holy Spirit. Satan can't stand against this divine power. He can stand against your strength, but he can't stand against God's power. Prayer is a central to

TRUE CONFESSIONS

One time when I was a teenager I dared the devil to attack me. I thought that just because I was a child of God there was no way that he could ever defeat me. I was wrong. Even children of God need to be walking in the power of God to win against Satan and sin. After triple-dog daring the devil, I went through a season of extreme trouble and temptation in my life. Why? I think God let Satan attack me to humble me and make me more dependent on Jesus. Lesson? Don't taunt the devil. Fight him in the power of God, not your own strength.

submitting to God. It's as you pray that you are submitting to his plan and purpose for your life. Like Jesus in the Garden of Gethsemane, you are declaring "Not my will, but your will be done." Submitting to God can be a sweaty, painful process, but it is the first step to defeating the devil. Secondly, you resist the devil. That means you push back, say "no," and refuse to give in to his bully words. When you submit to God and resist the devil he will run away from you every time, guaranteed.

Don't worry. He'll be back soon. That's okay. You'll be waiting to shove him in the chest once again in the power of God. Here's some encouragement from Scripture:

> Finally, be strong in the Lord and in his mighty power. Put on the full armor of God so that you can take your stand against the devil's schemes. For our struggle is not against flesh and blood, but against the rulers, against the authorities, against the powers of this dark world and against the spiritual forces of evil in the heavenly realms. (Ephesians 6:10-12)

I SAW THE SIGN

When I was 12 years old my youth leader, Tim Sanchez, gave me a morbid homework assignment that impressed upon me the seriousness of the spiritual battle that must be waged for lost souls. He told me to go to a local shopping mall on a Saturday afternoon and just sit on a bench at a busy section and watch people for 30 minutes. As I watched them I was supposed to imagine a small sign on their foreheads with the words "Bound for Hell" written across it. This whole thing sounded kind of weird to me, but I did it anyway.

I walked to the Westminster Mall, which was only a mile or so away from my house. Once in, I made my way around the mall for a few minutes trying to find the best place to sit down and begin my "homework." Once I found the right spot I sat down, settled in, and started looking at people intently, trying to imagine those eerie words scrawled across the foreheads of those who passed by. At first I felt stupid and self-conscious. People were watching me watch them and it felt uncomfortable. But in a few minutes I was well into my imagination exercise.

In those 30 minutes my life changed forever.

For 1,800 seconds I watched young and old, geeks and freaks, herds of nerds and flocks of jocks, blue-haired elderly women and blue-haired pierced skaters, swaggering mall security guards and staggering old men, moms trying to catch

CAN I GET A WITNESS?

My name is Andrea! I am 17 years old and from Stewartville, Minnesota. I really wanted to try talking to my friends [about Jesus]. I began praying and about a week later a friend from work just sat down and began telling me that he was really down and a lot of bad stuff was going on in his life. He continued to tell me how he was going to go home that night and get drunk so that he could forget about all of his problems. I thought—perfect opportunity to talk to him about God. But then the enemy came in and started telling me he won't listen, he's not going to care, he's probably going to go off and tell all the other guys at work what I said and make fun of me. But I remembered that all those thoughts were just the enemy trying to stop me, so I said a little prayer in my head asking God to give me strength to speak up and I did. About a month later he started to go to my youth group and he accepted Jesus Christ. After that he talked his brother into coming too. I learned not to listen to the enemy and how to recognize when the thoughts are mine and when they're the enemy. We can fight the enemy with God's help.

their toddlers on the run and dads trying to catch a nap on the benches. Not only did I imagine these people bound for a literal hell, I imagined their lives, apart from Christ, as a living hell. This was the closest I ever came to understanding Matthew 9:36, "When he saw the crowds, he had compassion on them, because they were harassed and helpless, like sheep without a shepherd." Jesus had His own imagination exercise. He envisioned the throngs of people that were following Him as sheep without a shepherd . . . scared, confused, and in danger.

That word "compassion" means to suffer with, to enter into somebody else's pain. That's what happened to Jesus on the hillside 2,000 years ago and me at the mall 27 years ago. It's almost as though God peeled back the curtain and allowed me to feel their hurts and see their pain. I imagined their lives without Christ and their afterlives without Christ and it broke my heart.

I never viewed people the same after that. I still see the sign. When I'm at the airport waiting in the security line I see the sign. When I'm sitting in traffic and turn to see the guy in the car next to me I see the sign. When I'm standing in front of thousands of screaming teenagers at a Dare 2 Share Conference I see the sign. When I'm sitting at a Starbucks (like I am now) and see the man next to me sipping his latte and looking out the window (like he is now) I see the sign. I can't get it out of my brain.

The sign keeps me up at night, wakes me up in the middle of the night and gets me out of bed in the morning. It drives me to prayer. It drives me to do what it takes to raise up an army of teenagers, youth leaders, parents, and pastors who see the sign too.

I saw the sign, and it opened up my eyes.

I challenge you to go to a busy mall on a crowded Saturday afternoon all by yourself and watch people for 30 minutes. Find a seat and see the "Bound for Hell" signs plastered on passing foreheads. Imagine how miserable their lives might be and their afterlives will be without Jesus. Feel their pain. Don't leave until you do. You're view of the spiritual battle that must be waged against the evil one will never be the same. When you are finished, write a letter to God recording your thoughts and feelings. Keep that letter as a reminder of this powerful and dramatic exercise of the imagination. It will help you stand against the evil one.

PART THREE:
REACHING OTHER WORLDVIEWS

STARBUCKS SPIRITUALITY

Right now as I sit in a Starbucks drinking a venti, sugar-free, vanilla-extra-shot Americano, I am reminded of a skit I wrote.

The drama opens with a line of people waiting to get their fix, but instead of customized caffeine concoctions, theirs was a have-it-your-way religious fix. One would order a *Carmel Cult Latte* with a *Hare Krishna Cookie* on the side. The next customer would be torn between the *Tai Chi Chai* and the *Mormon Frappuccino* (decaf only).

The only drink that wasn't served at this particular spirituality shop was a *Venti Jesus*. Your actualized, open-minded barista was open to giving you a quasi Jesus (Jesus with a shot of something else) but not straight Jesus. Why? Because once you had Him you would never thirst again. He was *the* way, *the* truth, *the* life, *the* drink.

Once you taste of Jesus, not only do you never thirst again, but you become suddenly possessed with a desire to get others to try this drink out. And if that happens too often, then Spiritual Starbucks is out of business for good.

This skit had a strong point that resonated with teens. Their world mixes spiritual beliefs like Starbucks mixes lattes, customized to their personal specifications. And that's a problem. Why? Because it assumes that it doesn't matter what you believe, only that you truly believe in *something*. If that's true, then maybe we are too hard on the villains of history. For instance, Hitler truly believed in something. His atrocities were simply natural outgrowths of what he sincerely believed.

If it doesn't matter what we believe, only that we believe, then morality is up for grabs depending on one's latte order. If we are the random results of an endless series of evolutionary mutations, then why not rape, murder, kill, and pillage?

But if we were made in the image of God for the glory of God, and if that same God who created us died for us and rose for us and lives in us, then why wouldn't we make it our life goal to make the world a better place? Why wouldn't we seek to honor those around us, even those who believe something radically different, because they too were made by God and for God? Why wouldn't we spend the rest of our lives serving Jesus in all His richness and taste to all those we come in contact with every day?

As I type these words a line is forming at Starbucks. It reminds me of how many people love the taste of coffee. How much more would people love the taste of Jesus if they would simply try Him out. What's more, Jesus never charges. He paid the price completely on the cross. Every other religion and belief system comes with a hefty charge, whether it be obeying some list of regulations, stopping some habit, starting some mantra, whatever. But this latte of life eternal is free, pre-purchased through the cross of Jesus.

And before He rose into heaven He gave us the charge to go into all the world and open up Jesus Latte franchises everywhere. He called us to be Bible Baristas and to raise up an army of baristas-in-training out of all nations. He commanded us to baptize them into this reality with three shots of transformation—the Father, Son, and Holy Spirit. And He reminded us that He will be right at our side as we stand behind the counter of political incorrectness delivering Jesus in all of His strength to a world in desperate need of better taste.

What does all this mean as you share your faith with all your friends who hang out at Spiritual Starbucks? Realize their beliefs are probably a blended drink . . . a shot of Jesus and a few pumps of New Age or whatever.

Help them understand what Jesus meant when He said, "I am the way and the truth and the life. No one can come to the Father except through me" (John 14:6).

"Venti Jesus, please!"

What religious beliefs are your friends concocting their spiritual latte from? Just having a basic understanding of the belief systems your friends may be choosing from can help you reach out to them and have real conversation. The next 13 chapters describe belief systems you may encounter at school, at the mall, online, at the gym, or anywhere people hang out and talk about life. All of the personal stories in the following chapters are true stories, though in some cases people's names and certain details of their stories have been changed to protect the privacy of the individuals involved. These stories are not meant to stereotype or degrade any certain group. I offer them to you as a way to personalize these belief systems and allow you to benefit from my own experience of sharing my faith in Jesus with others. Remember that some of those you encounter may take their latte straight up while others may be combining a shot of this and a few pumps of that to concoct their own special blend of spirituality. So ask questions, listen carefully, and customize your dialogue to fit each individual.

ALISHA THE AGNOSTIC

Alisha is smart and knows the Bible extremely well. Although she had a pretty religious background, she'd been in trouble with the law over the last few years for drugs and such. In her house growing up, she had to abide by a whole bunch of rules but was not taught about having an intimate relationship with God. This and some other influences caused her to rebel. Eventually her rebellion led to agnosticism.

As I shared with Alisha again and again, she was very open to discussion. She shared with me her doubts about God, Jesus, the Bible—everything that she had been raised to believe and embrace. She became more and more receptive to the gospel but still has a whole lot of questions. I'm still communicating with her and praying that she will come to embrace the real Christ, not the religious Jesus that her parents pushed on her. I pray she'll come to know the real, relevant, and powerful Jesus of the Bible!

BASIC DESCRIPTION

Alisha the Agnostic feels that God's existence can't be proven or disproven based on available evidence. For Alisha to believe in God or any kind of deity, she would need logical and rational proof. This is what makes Alisha different from Andy the Atheist (see chapter 25): She would most likely be open to the idea of God's existence if sufficient proof is offered. Alisha is similar to Andy in that they both deny the existence of a heaven/hell/spiritual world. Alisha would definitely not consider her agnostic beliefs a "religion"; rather, she would say they are concepts.

COMMON MISCONCEPTIONS

- Alisha's group is the same as atheists.

- Alisha's beliefs come from being an indecisive, unintelligent person.
- Alisha's beliefs are a compromise between believing/not believing in God.

THREE FASCINATING FACTS

- The word "agnostic" literally means "without knowledge." What they mean is that there is insufficient knowledge to "prove" there is a God.
- The title "agnostic" was coined by a famous English biologist named Thomas Huxley.
- For many years it was illegal to be an agnostic in France, and for this crime a person would receive the death sentence.

THINGS WE PROBABLY AGREE ON

- Alisha believes that much truth can be discovered.
- Alisha believes that people should treat each other with fairness and justice.
- Alisha believes in being a good person.

THINGS WE PROBABLY DISAGREE ON

- Alisha wants irrefutable proof for the existence of God, whereas God requires that we have faith in Him (Hebrews 11:1-3).
- Alisha believes that all people are born basically good, whereas the Bible teaches that all people are born with a predisposition toward sin (Psalm 51:5).
- Alisha does not believe in hell, but thinks there could be

some kind of heaven, whereas the Bible teaches the existence of both heaven and hell (Matthew 3:16; Luke 12:5).

SUGGESTED CONVERSATION STARTERS

- What would "proof" for God's existence look like to you?
- Are there things you believe in that have not been proven to you?
- Have you ever thought about the possibility that you might be wrong? (Be ready to answer this question yourself!)

A COMPLIMENT TO USE

- I really appreciate your honest questions. Too many times Christians aren't honest enough to ask the harder questions about life and God.

INTERESTING QUOTES

- "I don't know & you don't either."—militant agnostic, bumper sticker
- "I do not consider it an insult, but rather a compliment to be called an agnostic. I do not pretend to know where many ignorant men are sure—that is all that agnosticism means."—Clarence Darrow at the Scopes trial, 1925[1]

OTHER TIPS/SUGGESTIONS

- Speak as though there is a God and you may find them speaking as though they believe that because according to Romans 1:20 down deep inside, everyone does.
- Try and stick to the issue of what "proof" is for God and

how He has made Himself known through creation and science.

- Agnostics tend to look at Christians as intellectually inferior, so be sure to have your ideas and discussion points well thought out.
- Christians sometimes come across as superior to agnostics, so be sure to maintain a respectful and gracious attitude.

FOR FURTHER RESEARCH:

- www.dare2share.org/agnostics
- *The Case for Christ: Student Edition* by Lee Strobel

ANDY THE ATHEIST

I met Andy on a camping trip in the mountains. Out of the seven students we took, Andy was among the most vocal. A devout atheist, he had been raised in a family that didn't go to church or believe in God. His arguments ranged from "Well, if God is so good, then why does He allow suffering in the world" to questions like "Why would God send a devout Muslim to hell just because he didn't believe in Jesus?"

While I answered Andy straight from the Bible, he didn't trust in Christ as his Savior that week. He did, however, by his own admission "come closer" than he had ever before to considering the possibility that God exists. Andy agreed to read *The Case for Christ* by Lee Strobel and keep an open mind to the possibility that God could exist and that Christianity could be true.

Pray for Andy to believe.

BASIC DESCRIPTION

Andy does not believe in the existence of God, a supreme being, or any other spiritual beings for that matter. In his opinion this physical universe has always existed, and when a person dies, he or she ceases to exist forever. Andy most likely finds meaning in life through relationships and accomplishments.

COMMON MISCONCEPTIONS

- Andy hates or strongly dislikes all Christians.
- Andy hasn't thought through his position.
- Because Andy doesn't believe in God, he necessarily feels purposeless and lives immorally.

THREE FASCINATING FACTS

- Andy's group has founded organizations such as The Freedom from Religion Foundation and Internet Infidels.
- Andy's group (on average) has a higher level of education than the general population.
- Andy's group once had a man named C. S. Lewis in it who later became a Christian and wrote *The Chronicles of Narnia* series and many other great books.

THINGS WE PROBABLY AGREE ON

- Andy believes in the basic value of all people.
- Andy believes that relationships are important.
- Andy believes that no one person has all the answers.

THINGS WE PROBABLY DISAGREE ON

- Andy does not believe that the Bible is the Word of God, whereas the Bible claims to be just that (2 Timothy 3:16) and proves this claim through hundreds of fulfilled prophecies (Acts 3:18).
- Andy does not believe God exists, whereas the Bible clearly affirms His existence (Exodus 3:14).
- Andy does not believe in heaven or hell, whereas the Bible teaches the existence of both (Matthew 3:16; Luke 12:5).

SUGGESTED CONVERSATION STARTERS

- Why have you chosen to not believe in the existence of God?

- Have you ever considered the possibility that you could be wrong about the existence of God?
- Do you think there is a difference between religion and a relationship with God? Why or why not?

A COMPLIMENT TO USE

- I appreciate the courage you must have in your heart. I don't think that I could face life and all of its hardships without belief in a loving and all-powerful God.

INTERESTING QUOTES

- "Give a man a fish, and you'll feed him for a day; give him a religion, and he'll starve to death while praying for a fish."—Timothy Jones[1]
- "It may be that our role on this planet is not to worship God, but to create him."—Arthur C. Clarke[2]
- "I'm sickened by all religions. Religion has divided people. I don't think there's any difference between the pope wearing a large hat and parading around with a smoking purse and an African painting his face white and praying to a rock."—Howard Stern[3]

OTHER TIPS/SUGGESTIONS

- This is perhaps the most difficult faith-sharing scenario in the world, so you will need to spend some time finding common ground and defining your terms.
- Oftentimes when talking to atheists they will "forget" that they don't believe in the existence of God. They'll say things like, "Well, if God is so good then why . . ." Gently

point out to them that according to Romans 1:18-22 everybody, down deep inside, believes in the existence of God but they push down that truth and try to deny it with human rationalizations.

- One of the key issues when sharing with an atheist is to establish that the Bible is God's Word, so be sure you can walk him or her through the evidences for this fact. As well, atheists love to point out all the "contradictions" in the Bible, so be careful not to get too sidetracked on this issue. The other key issue is the birth, death, and resurrection of Jesus Christ, so (again) be sure you have a thought-out line of reasoning when discussing this.

FOR FURTHER RESEARCH:

- www.dare2share.org/atheists
- *The Case for Christ: Student Edition* by Lee Strobel

BAILEY THE BUDDHIST

Bailey is my therapist (for my bicep, not my brain!). I met her after I tore or strained something in the tendon that connects my bicep to my bone. After a session or two we started talking about spirituality. When I found out she was a Buddhist, I shared with her how I was writing this book *Dare 2 Share* for teenagers. I explained how I was going to share about different religions and Bailey graciously gave me the Evangetips when it came to Buddhist beliefs. She even offered to get me some articles from their main Buddhist publication.

To be honest I was surprised at how open Bailey was to the story of Christianity. While she rejects it as being her truth, she nonetheless thinks it is a beautiful story.

My challenge is this: How do I convince her that the gospel is more than a fable in the periodic 15-minute ultrasound sessions (bicep, not the belly!)? Yesterday I dropped off *The Case for Christ* by Lee Strobel at her office. She had promised to read it and get back to me about her thoughts.

The conversation continues . . .

BASIC DESCRIPTION

Bailey's group can best be summed up by the term "religious atheist" because the American form of Buddhism is perfect for those who reject the idea of God, yet still seek after the history and tradition of religious experience. Buddhism also includes a strong emphasis on meditation, which gives Bailey a sense of inner peace. Bailey's ultimate goal is to achieve nirvana (not the band)—which is a state of being that is totally separated from individuality, negative emotions, and desires. The reason Buddhists seek this is because these things cause suffering and evil in the world, and force people into an endless cycle of birth/death/rebirth with bad karma. Buddhism also answers the question of suffering and evil in the world very simply: Bad people do bad things, so they pay for it in subsequent lives (i.e., karma).

Buddhists do not believe in a personal God, so there is no "church" or worship in Buddhism. Also, the concepts of forgiveness, heavenly hope, and final judgment are absent from Buddhism as well, so think of their worldview more as a philosophy than a "religion."

COMMON MISCONCEPTIONS

- Bailey believes that Buddha was God.
- Bailey worships in a temple.
- Bailey has a big belly and if you rub it you'll have good luck.

THREE FASCINATING FACTS

- Buddha himself was unsure about what happens after death.
- Many so-called "sayings" of Buddha were actually written 400 years after his death.
- The term "nirvana" literally means the "blowing out" of existence.

THINGS WE PROBABLY AGREE ON

- Bailey seeks inner peace.
- Bailey believes in life after death.
- Bailey is troubled by evil and suffering in the world.

THINGS WE PROBABLY DISAGREE ON

- Bailey does not believe in a personal God, whereas the Bible teaches not only His existence, but His personal concern as well (Psalm 46:10).

- Bailey believes in a repeated cycle of birth/death/rebirth, whereas the Bible teaches that we die only once, then face judgment for how we lived our lives (Hebrews 9:27).

- Bailey believes that Buddha showed the path to "salvation" (i.e., nirvana), whereas the Bible teaches that Jesus is the only way to heaven (John 14:6).

SUGGESTED CONVERSATION STARTERS

- What do you believe about what happens after death?

- Why is there evil and suffering in the world?

- Have you ever felt the need to be forgiven?

A COMPLIMENT TO USE

- One of the things I really appreciate about Buddhism is how it seeks peace. We have too much war and conflict in the world and not nearly enough peace.

INTERESTING QUOTES

- "Things are not what they appear to be: nor are they otherwise."—Buddha, Surangama Sutra[1]

- "The ultimate authority must always rest with the individual's own reason and critical analysis."—H. H. The 14th Dalai Lama[2]

OTHER TIPS/SUGGESTIONS

- Keep in mind that there are several different "versions" of Buddhism, so make sure you get a detailed explanation from your Buddhist friends about what they believe and why they believe it.

- Since Buddhists seek to experience salvation (nirvana) through a system of good deeds, make sure you explain that biblical salvation is a free gift received through faith in Jesus based on His death, burial, and resurrection.

- Because many Buddhists are Asian or of Asian descent, you need to be sensitive toward the cultural differences that may exist. If you aren't, it will be difficult to establish a friendship with them, and as a result, it will be more complicated to share your faith.

FOR FURTHER RESEARCH:

- www.dare2share.org/buddhists
- *Sharing Your Faith with a Buddhist* by M. S. Thirumalai, Madasamy Thirumalai

DANIELLE THE DEIST

I met Danielle at the mall. She was there with a friend and I just felt compelled to share Christ with her. When I asked her whether or not she was going to heaven when she died, she said that she hoped so, but didn't know for sure. I asked her if I could share with her how she could know for sure from the Bible. She said yes. Her friend listened along intently.

Over the next few minutes I shared the gospel story with Danielle. She had always believed in some kind of God, but thought that if you were generally a good person (no matter which God you believed in) you would make it to heaven someday.

When she heard the gospel, that Jesus was not *a* way to heaven, but *the* way, *the* truth, and *the* life, she put her faith and trust in Christ right there in the shopping mall. She then looked at her friend with a knowing smile. She said, "I told you so." Wondering what they were talking about, I asked her what was going on. She shared with me that they had been at the mall earlier in the day and had left to go back to her house. Once there, Danielle shared that something was telling her to go back to the mall. At first her friend thought she was weird, but Danielle finally convinced her that something was going to happen there. That something was our conversation, and Danielle knew it.

This all shows that God is working on the hearts of the Danielles out there who believe in some kind of vague, impersonal God. God is preparing the way for your conversation with them whether they be a stranger in the mall or a friend at your school.

BASIC DESCRIPTION

Many people with Deist beliefs may have never actually heard of the word "Deist," but they unknowingly hold to the basic

Deist belief that there is a God, but He's not really knowable and He's not involved in human affairs. They take the position that there is no one way to believe when it comes to God and spirituality. Most Deists believe that the vast majority of people go to heaven because most people are basically good, and if there is a hell, only really bad people like Adolph Hitler and other mass murderers go there.

The bottom line is that while many Deists might have considered themselves "spiritual," by no means would they say they are "religious." Basically, the Bible and church are irrelevant to them because they play no significant role in helping meet their goals of finding significant relationships and making significant money. For Deists, God is like a disinterested observer, out there somewhere, but not interested in them.

COMMON MISCONCEPTIONS

- Deists only care about themselves.
- Deists don't care about spiritual things.
- Deists would never have set foot in a church building (studies show that most of the people out there would go if they were invited by a friend!).

THREE FASCINATING FACTS

- Deism is a reason-based faith that emphasizes experience and free thought rather than beliefs based on any holy texts.
- Deists often mix many different views of God together and see Him the way they want Him to be.
- Many people who have never heard the world "Deist" live

by the Deist belief that there is a God, but He's not really knowable and He's not an active part of their daily lives.

THINGS WE PROBABLY AGREE ON

- Deists believe God exists.
- Deists believe God gave humans the ability to reason.
- Deists believe God wants us to be good people.

THINGS WE PROBABLY DISAGREE ON

- Deist do not believe in absolute truth, whereas the Bible claims to be the inspired Word of God and therefore absolute truth (2 Timothy 3:16).
- Deist believe that reason and observation tell us all we need to know about God, and that there is no possibility of a personal relationship with the God they see as the Architect of the Universe (Psalm 100:3).
- Deist do not believe that Jesus is the only way to heaven, whereas Jesus claims to be just that (John 14:6).

SUGGESTED CONVERSATION STARTERS

- What exactly are your spiritual beliefs? Would you share them with me?
- What do you think happens after we die?
- Have you ever considered the claim Jesus made that He is the only way to heaven?

A COMPLIMENT TO USE

- There have been a lot of very intelligent people who have held Deists beliefs, including many of America's forefathers like Benjamin Franklin and Thomas Jefferson.

chapter 33

NICOLE THE NEW AGER

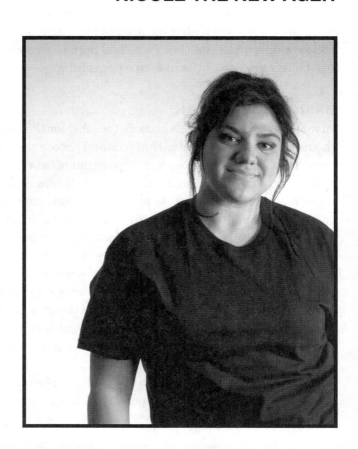

My wife introduced me to Nicole. She was young, pretty, and full-on New Age in her beliefs. She had crystals, practiced meditation, did Yoga—the whole bit. When my wife and I first started talking to her about Jesus she was very open-minded. After all, being open-minded is one of the unofficial tenets of New Age thought. It didn't take very long before she understood that the spiritual fulfillment she had been looking for in the New Age movement could only be found in Jesus. Not only did she come to Christ, she came to church with us. Pretty soon she began to share Jesus with those around her with a passion. It was awesome to see somebody who had been so steeped in New Age beliefs come to Christ in such a powerful way.

BASIC DESCRIPTION

In many ways, New Age has become the label for those who see themselves as highly spiritual but pick and choose their own personal beliefs from across a vast spectrum of belief systems such as Eastern mysticism, meditation, self-help, sustainable living and positive thinking, to name a few. New Agers seek to create "a spirituality without borders or confining dogmas."[1] Beliefs vary greatly depending upon individual preference. A New Ager may be into their horoscopes—or not. They may be into meditation—or not. They may be into environmentally sustainable living—or not. But most New Agers believe that humanity is evolving toward a "new age" of peaceful prosperity. They view themselves as non-religious, yet highly spiritual people who strive to be in touch with both the cosmos and with their inner selves.

Most New Agers do not believe in God as a person; rather, they feel God is a term for an impersonal force, energy, or consciousness. As far as the afterlife, most New Agers are similar to Wiccans in that they believe in karma and reincarnation, which is the conviction that "what goes around comes around," and that our souls are eternal and go through a series of "incarnations" (i.e., enter into flesh) as they evolve. Some New Agers may even accept the reality of some kind of heaven where everybody is welcome.

COMMON MISCONCEPTIONS
- Each New Ager holds the same beliefs as every other New Ager.
- New Agers have no respect for Jesus.
- New Agers have a good understanding of Christianity.

THREE FASCINATING FACTS
- New Agers have teachers called "Metaphysical Ministers."
- New Agers believe that "God" is a combination of everyone and everything in their spiritual interconnectedness.
- Many New Age beliefs come from an attempt to merge Eastern religions (Hinduism, Buddhism, etc.) with a Western lifestyle (success, positive thinking, etc.).

THINGS WE PROBABLY AGREE ON
- New Agers believe that there is some truth in the Bible.
- New Agers believe that Jesus Christ existed and was a powerful, enlightened being.
- Many New Agers believe in an eternal soul and some kind of afterlife.

THINGS WE PROBABLY DISAGREE ON

- Many New Agers believe in reincarnation, whereas the Bible teaches that people only die once (Hebrews 9:27).

- New Agers do not believe in the biblical concept of sin or the need for forgiveness from sin, whereas the Bible affirms that everyone on earth is sinful and needs to be forgiven (Romans 3:23).

- New Agers do not believe in a judgment day where those who trusted Christ will receive rewards and enter heaven, and those who rejected Christ will be sentenced to hell, whereas the Bible teaches that this day is real (Revelation 20:11-15).

SUGGESTED CONVERSATION STARTERS

- What do you believe about Jesus Christ?

- Do you think that a person's spiritual beliefs should be a total leap of faith, or should they have some level of evidence for being true?

- What if your belief system is wrong?

A COMPLIMENT TO USE

- I really appreciate that you have a spiritual view of all of life and nature. That's something we have in common!

INTERESTING QUOTES

- "The New Age movement may well reflect the future face of Western religion." —Nevill Drury[1]

- "The purpose of our lives is to give birth to the best which is within us." —Marianne Williamson[2]

OTHER TIPS/SUGGESTIONS

- Don't expect every New Ager to believe the same thing, so make sure you let your New Age friend clearly express his or her views.

- Clearly define your terms. New Agers use a lot of words that are similar to Christianity but have completely different meanings, such as "Christ consciousness" and "God."

- Try to establish some kind of common ground with New Agers through conversation. Some examples of this could be the search for purpose and value, the reality of the afterlife, and the belief that Jesus Christ existed.

- When appropriate, point out the weaknesses in the New Age worldview, as this may create an interest in Christianity. Some of the weaknesses include:

    1. The denial of sin . . . how do you explain evil?

    2. An impersonal god . . . if God is a combination of the spiritual connectedness of everyone, how can personal beings make up an impersonal force?

    3. Lack of evidence . . . where's the proof for reincarnation?

FOR FURTHER RESEARCH:

- www.dare2share.org/newagers
- *Confronting the New Age* by Douglas Groothuis

chapter 34

RYAN THE RELIGIOUS

Ryan was raised in a church that tended to preach a message that heaven could be achieved through good deeds rather than received by faith alone in Christ alone. One day Ryan was helping me with a building project and we got into a lengthy conversation about God and justice. He was questioning whether or not God was just and fair because of some tragedies that God had allowed in the world.

I shared with Ryan that it was the justice of God that sent Jesus to the cross. That captured his attention. He always thought that it was the love of God that propelled Jesus to die for the sins of mankind. I assured him that it was both the love and the justice of God. On that hot day working outside in the blazing Colorado sun, I explained that because God was perfect and demanded perfection, it took a perfect sacrifice (Jesus) to pay for the sins of fallen humanity. Although Ryan didn't trust in Christ as his Savior on the spot, we have had several conversations since. I'm still praying for Ryan to understand that it's not his good deeds that will get him to heaven, but faith in Jesus for the act of justice and love He committed on the cross for us!

BASIC DESCRIPTION

Ryan claims to be a Christian. But his brand of Christianity is mere religion and not a relationship with Jesus. His group goes by many names, but they have one thing in common: They are merely religious—meaning they are trying to get to heaven through a combination of faith and works. Ryan recognizes that Jesus died for his sins, but he feels he must also do good deeds in order to earn the right to go to heaven. These deeds would include (but are not limited to) things like baptism, going to church, helping the needy, and reading the Bible.

Ryan is not trusting in Christ alone for his salvation, which is why he feels it is necessary to rack up a list of spiritual accomplishments for judgment day.

COMMON MISCONCEPTIONS
- Ryan is angry, self-righteous, and judgmental.
- Ryan knows a lot about the Bible.
- Ryan is a true Christian just because he goes to church.

THREE FASCINATING FACTS
- The word "religion" originally meant "to bind back"—i.e., "bind" oneself back to God through good deeds.
- A Gallup Poll in 2010 found that 54% of Americans said that religion was "very important" in their lives.[1]
- A Google search for "religious" brings over 179 million results!

THINGS WE PROBABLY AGREE ON
- Religious people who go to church generally believe in God and Jesus.
- Religious people tend to be interested in spiritual things.
- Religious people usually believe the Bible is the Word of God.

THINGS WE PROBABLY DISAGREE ON
- Ryan believes that good works are necessary for entrance into heaven, whereas the Bible teaches that the gift of eternal life is by grace through faith alone (Ephesians 2:8-9).

- Ryan believes he can earn God's favor by performing good deeds, whereas the Bible teaches that our "good deeds" are like filthy rags in God's sight (Isaiah 64:6).
- Ryan believes that the Bible is God's Word but shouldn't be taken too literally, whereas the Bible teaches that every word of it is inspired by God and should all be taken seriously (2 Timothy 3:16).

SUGGESTED CONVERSATION STARTERS

- If you stood before God and He asked you why He should let you into heaven, what would you say?
- If good works are necessary for salvation, how many do you have to do? What if you don't do enough?
- How would you describe your relationship with God?

A COMPLIMENT TO USE

- Some of the greatest achievements of mankind, whether in the world of sciences, arts, or humanitarian service, have been done by religiously devoted individuals.

INTERESTING QUOTES

- "But those who depend on the law to make them right with God are under his curse, for the Scriptures say, 'All who rely on observing the law are under a curse, for it is written: "Cursed is everyone who does not continue to do everything written in the Book of the Law"'"—Galatians 3:10
- "Then the Lord said to him, 'Now then, you Pharisees clean the outside of the cup and dish, but inside you are full of greed and wickedness'"—Luke 11:39

OTHER TIPS/SUGGESTIONS

- Focus on the inconsistency of a works-based approach to getting into heaven—what is the standard for a "good" work? What if you did it with the wrong motive—does it still count? How many good works are necessary for salvation?

- Religious people have a degree of doubt about their salvation, so try and bring up the true believer's assurance of salvation.

- Ask them to show you where the Bible teaches a person can be saved from hell and enter heaven through their good works.

FOR FURTHER RESEARCH:

- www.dare2share.org/religious
- *The Grace Awakening* by Chuck Swindoll

chapter 35

SID THE SATANIST

I met Sid at the mall. Since I went to a Christian school during my high school years, I had to go out to "create" relationships with teenagers who would hang out at the mall week after week. It was there where I met Sid, a self-proclaimed Satanist.

It surprised me to know that Sid knew the Bible very well. He could quote large passages from memory. Every time I saw Sid we would talk. While he was cemented deeply into his belief system, he was very open to discuss and debate the issues of spirituality with me in a cordial way.

One night I walked into a Denny's and heard Sid yell out to me. He was sitting in the smoking section of Denny's puffing away with all of his Satanic buddies. He called me over and I came. He made me sit down and in his words give his friends "the speech." I was surprised that Sid wanted me to share the gospel with his friends, but I gladly obliged. For the next few minutes I shared the gospel with the five or six who were tucked in the big booth with Sid. Afterward while everybody was chattering about what I'd said (mostly mockingly), I leaned over to Sid and asked him if he was reconsidering his beliefs. He looked me squarely in the eyes and said, "Yes, I am."

I haven't seen Sid since. But I believe the Spirit of God was on the verge of catching him after a long chase through the abyss called Satanism. I hope to see Sid one day in heaven!

BASIC DESCRIPTION

Sid's group can vary widely in their Satanic beliefs and practices, but most are self-taught Satanists who for one reason or another became interested in the occult and decided to delve deeper into it. Sid practices rituals designed to bring him power and control over the world around him. These rituals include but are not limited to:

incantations, Satanic ceremonies, and animal sacrifices.

Sid and his group despise anything to do with Christianity. They see believers as weak-minded people who use Jesus as a crutch. As well, Sid will tend to go for whatever brings shock value—be it clothes, music, or other cultural options that carry a Satanic theme.

COMMON MISCONCEPTIONS

- Sid has thoroughly thought through his belief system.
- Sid believes just like all other Satanists.
- Sid shares the same belief system as Wiccans.

THREE FASCINATING FACTS

- The majority of Satanists are "dabblers"—meaning they are not fully immersed in it.
- One form of Satanism called "LaVey" Satanism denies the existence of Satan himself! LaVey Satanists are atheists who deny the existence of God, Satan, demons, and angels. The "Satan" that they worship is the pursuit of personal pleasure. Although most Satanists are self-styled "dabblers," the LaVey vein claims to be the true Satanic church and is an officially recognized religion in America.
- The Bible describes Satan as having the ability to disguise himself as an "angel of light" (2 Corinthians 11:14).

THINGS WE PROBABLY AGREE ON

- Sid believes that there is a God.
- Sid believes in a spiritual world complete with angels and demons.

- Sid believes that God and Satan are in a cosmic battle for the souls of mankind.

THINGS WE PROBABLY DISAGREE ON

- Sid believes true power and freedom are found in Satanism, whereas the Bible teaches that following Satan enslaves a person (2 Timothy 2:25-27).
- Sid believes that occult practices are basically harmless, whereas the Bible teaches that they are incredibly dangerous and forbidden by God (Deuteronomy 18:9-11).
- Sid believes that in the end, Satan and his followers will be victorious over God, whereas the Bible teaches that God defeats Satan (Revelation 20:7-10).

SUGGESTED CONVERSATION STARTERS

- What influenced your decision to become a Satanist?
- What positive impact has Satanism had on your life?
- Have you ever considered the possibility that in the end God wins?

A COMPLIMENT TO USE

- I've got to appreciate the unflinching boldness that you show in declaring yourself a Satanist in a nation where the average person describes himself as a Christian. You have a lot of courage to do that!

INTERESTING QUOTES

- "Every religion in the world that has destroyed people is based on love."—Anton LaVey, *The Satanic Bible*[1]

- "Satan himself masquerades as an angel of light. It is not surprising, then, if his servants masquerade as servants of righteousness. Their end will be what their actions deserve."—2 Corinthians 11:14-15

OTHER TIPS/SUGGESTIONS

- Satanists typically have a built-in hatred for Christianity, so it is key that you earn the right to be heard through developing a solid relationship. Never come across as judgmental.

- Help them understand the difference between religion/religious people and Jesus Christ. Bring up the biblical stories of how Jesus opposed religious and self-righteous people all the time.

- Try and help them see that Satanism is a trap, and true freedom is found in trusting Christ.

FOR FURTHER RESEARCH:

- www.dare2share.org/satanists
- *Satanism* by Bob Passantino, Dr. Alan W. Gomes

chapter 36

WILLOW THE WICCAN

Willow lived in my neighborhood. Almost every month a group would arrive at her house, frequently gathering in her backyard around the light of a bonfire. While many of my neighbors despised her, I tried to wave at her every time I saw her. She knew that I was a preacher and she knew that I knew she was into Wicca.

Before I shared the gospel with her I wanted to establish a firm notion in her head that I was a nice guy. I accomplished that with smiles and waves and an occasional "how are you?" conversation. I was praying for an opportunity to lovingly bring up the gospel with her.

One winter day, my wife and I heard something rustling in the backyard. At first I thought it was some kind of wild animal, a fox or something. As I looked around I saw what it was, a ferret that had escaped its home was trying to find a place in our window well to stay warm. I put some gloves on and gently grabbed it, surprised by its tameness.

I then took the next step of going door-to-door in my neighborhood to find out whose it was. As I went to house after house, I got the sinking feeling in my stomach that maybe it was Willow's. To be honest, I hoped it wasn't. Though I was friendly to Willow from a distance, I wasn't in the mood to have a Jesus conversation at her doorstep on a cold, wintry day.

As I knocked on her door she almost immediately swung it open, startling me. She immediately yelled in excitement that I had found her lost ferret. She was so excited and thankful that she gave me some homemade pickles. She then admitted to me that I was the only neighbor who was nice to her.

Here was my chance to share Jesus, but I blew it. I thanked her for the pickles and said good-bye, justifying to myself that the door was now open to share my faith and that I would do it at a more convenient time. That time never came because soon after, she suddenly moved out. I missed the opportunity that God had given me to share with Willow and I have regretted it ever since.

BASIC DESCRIPTION

Most Wiccans have a deep love and respect for nature and creation, but do not recognize or even believe in God as the Creator. Wiccans believe in a god and goddess, as well as a multitude of divine entities (such as spirits) and connect with them through rituals. Wicca gives its followers power in casting spells and in controlling their lives. The majority of Wiccans practice what they call "white magic"—meaning magic that is intended to do good.

Wiccans are strong believers in karma and reincarnation—that is, the conviction that "what goes around comes around," and that our souls are eternal and go through a series of "incarnations" (i.e., enter into flesh) as they evolve.

COMMON MISCONCEPTIONS

- Willow and her friends are witches who howl at the moon and cast dark spells.
- Willow believes in Satan.
- Willow actively tries to convert people to her beliefs.

THREE FASCINATING FACTS

- Wicca is also known as a "neo-pagan" religion and has been around in one form or another for thousands of years.

- The initiation training for Wiccans in a coven takes about a year to complete.
- Many Wiccans believe that the god they worship is Jehovah and/or Allah.

THINGS WE PROBABLY AGREE ON

- Wiccans believe in a supreme being.
- Wiccans believe in the spiritual world.
- Wiccans believe in life after death.

THINGS WE PROBABLY DISAGREE ON

- Wiccans do not believe in sin or see a need for forgiveness, whereas the Bible affirms that everyone on earth is sinful and needs to be forgiven (Romans 3:23).
- Wiccans do not believe in heaven or hell, whereas the Bible teaches the existence of both (Matthew 3:16; Luke 12:5).
- Wiccans believe there is a "good" type of magic, whereas the Bible warns that all magic/witchcraft/sorcery is evil and a serious offense to God (Deuteronomy 18:10-12).

SUGGESTED CONVERSATION STARTERS

- Have you had any other experiences with religion or religious groups? If so, what happened?
- What do Wiccans believe about Christians?
- Have you ever considered the idea that the Creator of the universe came to visit and even die for His creation?

A COMPLIMENT TO USE

- One of the things I really respect about Wicca is how it so deeply respects life and nature.

INTERESTING QUOTES

- "Sorry I missed church, I was busy practicing witch-craft."—bumper sticker
- "Our only animosity towards Christianity, or towards any other religion or philosophy of life, is to the extent that its institutions have claimed to be 'the only way' and have sought to deny freedom to others and to suppress other ways of religious practice and belief."—13 Principles of Wiccan Belief[1]

OTHER TIPS/SUGGESTIONS

- One of the biggest obstacles you will have with Wiccans is their conviction that they don't need forgiveness. Because of this, focus on how all people have broken God's perfect law by going through the Ten Commandments (see chapter 11). You can also use the "three sins a day" illustration, which goes like this:

   Most people think they are pretty good, because they can usually think of someone worse. Would you say that a person who only messed up (lied, gossiped, lusted, etc.) three times a day would be good? Most would say "yes," but think about it—if I only sin three times a day, that's over a thousand sins a year. That means if I live to be 70, I will have broken God's laws over 70,000 times!

- Wiccans typically aren't convinced that Christians are caring/loving people, so change that perception by being Christlike in everything you do!

FOR FURTHER RESEARCH:

- www.dare2share.org/wiccans
- *When Someone You Love Is Wiccan: A Guide to Witchcraft and Paganism for Concerned Friends, Nervous Parents, and Curious Co-Workers* by Carl McColman

Chapter 1

1. Pan Hui, Sonja Buchegger, "Groupthink and Peer Pressure: Social Influence in Online Social Network Groups," asonam, pp.53-59, International Conference on Advances in Social Network Analysis and Mining, 2009.

Chapter 2

1. HePrayed.com, Quotes, William Booth, http://www. heprayed.com/quotes.asp?filterAuthor =William+Booth&f ilterSubject=All&filterOrder=rating+desc.

2. Adapted from Greg Stier, *You're Next* (Carol Stream, Ill.: Tyndale House Publishers, Inc., 2007), pages 65-70.

Chapter 4

1. Pan Hui, Sonja Buchegger, "Groupthink and Peer Pressure: Social Influence in Online Social Network Groups," asonam, pp.53-59, International Conference on Advances in Social Network Analysis and Mining, 2009.

Chapter 16

1. Adapted from Greg Stier, *Outbreak* (Chicago, Ill.: Moody Publishers, 2006), pages 171-172.

Chapter 24

1. BrainyMedia.com, "Brainy Quote," *Clarence Darrow Quotes*, http://brainyquotes.com/quotes/quotes/c/ clarenceda103622.html.

Chapter 25

1. BrainyMedia.com, "Brainy Quote," *Timothy Jones Quotes*, www.brainyquote.com/quotes/quotes/t/timothyjon176701.html.

2. BrainyMedia.com, "Brainy Quote," *Arthur C. Clarke Quotes*, www.brainyquote.com/quotes/quotes/a/arthurccl161414.html.

3. ThinkExist, "Thinkexist.com," *Howard Stern Quotes*, http://en.thinkexist.com/quotation/i-m_sickened_by_all_religions-religion_has/209457.html.

Chapter 26

1. A View on Buddhism, "Buddhist Quotes and Sayings," http://buddhism.kalachakranet.org/resources/buddhist_quotes.html. Ibid.

Chapter 27

1. ThinkExist, "Thinkexist.com," *Benjamin Franklin Quotes*, http://thinkexist.com/quotation/god_helps_those_who_help_themselves/154978.html.

Chapter 28

1. Katha Upanishad, *The Aquarian Theosophist* 4, no.7 (May 2004): p. 7, www.teosofia.com/Docs/vol-4-7-supplement.pdf.

2. OneLittleAngel.com, "Hinduism Upanishads Quotes," www.onelittleangel.com/wisdom/quotes/book.asp?mc=215; quote #6.

Chapter 29

1. Watchtower: Official Web Site of Jehovah Witnesses, "Membership and Publishing Statistics," www.jw-media. org/people/statistics.htm.

2. *1939 Yearbook of Jehovah's Witnesses* (Brooklyn: Watch Tower Bible and Tract Society, 1939), p. 85.

3. Watchtower Official Site of Jehovah Witnesses, "Is God Always Superior to Jesus?" www.watchtower.org/library/ ti/index.htm?article=article_06.htm.

Chapter 30

1. SimpleToRemember.com, "Judaism Online," *Jewish Quotes*, www.simpletoremember.com/vitals/quotes.htm.

Chapter 31

1. Newsroom.LDS.org, "Facts and Stats," www. http://beta-newsroom.lds.org/facts-and-stats#noid.

2. Joseph Smith, *History of the Church*, Vol. 4 (Salt Lake City, Utah: 1978), p. 461. No publisher given.

3. Brigham Young, *Journal of Discourses*, Vol. 3 (Salt Lake City, Utah: 1967), p. 247. No publisher given.

Chapter 32

1. The Pew Forum on Religion and Public Life, "Mapping the Global Muslim Population," http://pewforum.org/ Muslim/Mapping-the-Global-Muslim-Population.aspx.

2. Abdullah Yusuf Ali, *The Meaning of the Holy Qur'an* (Beltsville, Md: Amana Publications, 2003), p. 251.

3. Islamic Invitation Center, "Who are the Muslims?" www. islamicinvitationcentre.com/articles/Introduction/fastest/ fastest_planet.html.#Anchor-AB-38902.

Chapter 33

1. Nevill Drury, *The New Age: Searching for the Spiritual Self* (London: Thames and Hudson, 2004)

2. Nevill Drury, *The New Age: The History of a Movement* (London: Thames & Hudson, 2004).

3. Starlark, "New Age Quotes," www.starlark.com/ NewAgeQuotes.html.

Chapter 34

1. Gallup, "Near-Record High See Religion Losing Influence in America" December 29, 2010, www.gallup.com/ poll/145409/Near-Record-High-Religion-Losing- Influence-America.aspx.

Chapter 35

1. Think Exist, "Thinkexist.com," *Anton LaVey Quotes*, http://en.thinkexist.com/quotes/anton_lavey.

Chapter 36

1. The Internet Sacred Text Archive, "Principles of Wiccan Beliefs," www.sacred-texts.com/bos/bos056.htm.

ABOUT THE AUTHOR

Greg Stier is the founder and president of Dare 2 Share Ministries International (D2S). Since 1991, Greg has impacted the lives of tens of thousands of Christian teenagers through Dare 2 Share events. Greg combines amazing true-life stories and side-splitting humor to communicate sound Biblical truth in a way that not only inspires teenagers, but motivates them to action. He and his team are committed to mobilize teenagers to relationally and relentlessly reach this young generation for Christ. He is the author of ten books and numerous resources, including *Venti Jesus Please* and *Reach Out...Don't Freak Out.*

D2S also provides free online resources and a variety of curriculum, books and other training resources for students and youth leaders. For more information about Dare 2 Share's resources and training conferences, please visit www. dare2share.org. Look for the free resource Soul Fuel and sign up to receive it online.

EVANGELISM BOOKS
FROM DARE 2 SHARE

INZANE by Zane Black

Zane's life story will inspire you to live for Christ!
Told in his raw, honest, conversational style,
InZane...Totally Stoked on this Jesus Dude captures
Zane's journey from a party boy to a committed
Christian. His story will keep you turning the page,
and at the same time challenge you to put Jesus at
the center of your life.

LIFE IN 6 WORDS...the outreach book
by Greg Stier

Using the six words of the GOSPEL—God, Our,
Sins, Paying, Everyone, Life—*Life in 6 Words* clearly
communicate Jesus' invitation to trust in Him.
This short, compelling, visually dynamic book is a
perfect evangelism tool for relationally engaging
others with the gospel of grace.

VENTI JESUS PLEASE by Greg Stier

For anyone who's ever wondered about spiritual
things, listening in on this conversation between
three high school friends could open up a whole
new world of possibilities. A perfect tool to reach
an unbelieving teenager.

These books are available at **www.dare2share.org**

MORE GREAT RESOURCES
FROM DARE 2 SHARE

EVANGELISM TRAINING EVENTS

Dare 2 Share provides 2-day student evangelism training conferences, as well as youth leader training events. Current events schedule available at **www.dare2share.org/conferences**

ONLINE EVANGELISM RESOURCES

Live THE Cause in community by joining the conversation on the Dare 2 Share page at **www.facebook.com/livethecause**

Plus, over 1,000 free resources are available at **www.dare2share.org** to help you relationally and relentlessly share the gospel and live THE Cause by making disciples who make disciples.

DARE 2 SHARE IN YOUR INBOX

Sign up for Soul Fuel from Dare 2 Share and get weekly emails that use music, movies, TV and trends to inspire you to live for THE Cause of Christ! Sign up to receive Soul Fuel weekly at **www.dare2share.org/students**

These resources are available at **www.dare2share.org**

CURRICULUM
FROM DARE 2 SHARE

LIFE IN 6 WORDS: THE GOSPEL EXPLORED
featuring Greg Stier and Jason Petty ("Propaganda")

This 7-week DVD curriculum dives into the theology of the gospel message, unpacking core terms and concepts every follower of Jesus needs to grasp to fully understand the good news. This curriculum will challenge your teenagers with truths that have the power to transform their own lives as well as enable them to more fully explain God's great story.

GOSPEL JOURNEY MAUI
featuring Greg Stier

Relational, relevant and edgy, the *GOSPEL Journey Maui* reality series is all about real questions and real conversations. Seven young strangers with very different spiritual worldviews and a preacher/wannabe-surfer hung out for an entire week in Maui, diving into life's biggest questions: Is there a higher power? What is the purpose of life? What happens when we die? and more... Ultimately it boiled down to this: Can everyone be rights? Follow the cast on their journey to discover the truth.

GOSPEL JOURNEY featuring Greg Stier

In the first *GOSPEL Journey* reality series, Greg Stier takes seven students into the Rocky Mountains for a journey through the gospel message using the G-O-S-P-E-L acronym. This unscripted adventure uses challenges like white water rafting and rock climbing along with powerful illustrations from nature and life to lead seven strangers on a riveting journey toward Jesus.

These resources are available at **www.dare2share.org**

Join other youth leaders at **www.facebook.com/dare2share**